BRA

"Life isn't easy. If it was, there would be no need for this book, but it isn't. Life is full of challenges and changes. You're going to have to be brave, and this book may be just what you need to find the help God gives!"

Paul Harcourt, national leader, New Wine England

"I read Brave at a time when our family was facing some tough challenges. It was like medicine for me, and I would prescribe it to anybody who needs hope, practical advice, inspiring stories, and well-researched insight. Debbie is a nurse, a teacher and a support to many, and she brings her knowledge, experience and personal courage to every page. This is a book I will be returning to and recommending many times in the days and months ahead. After all, we all need another dose of Brave from time to time."

Cathy Madavan, author of *Digging for Diamonds* and member of the Spring Harvest Planning Group

"Debbie Duncan is an ordinary woman following an extraordinary God. She and her family have faced illness, bereavement and other hardships that seem staggering from the sidelines. How has she coped? Through being brave and resilient, with the help of the Holy Spirit. In Brave, she shares stories and tips from her extraordinary journey, which will encourage and strengthen your faith in God."

Amy Boucher Pye, author of *Finding Myself in Britain*

"Brave is such a helpful book! In fact, it's more than that, as it's full of relatable stories of people who have had to face, or are currently facing, deep disappointments in various ways, yet found the ability to be 'brave'. What I love about this book is that not only do the stories bring to life things we all face at various times, but Debbie gives wonderful and insightful teaching on how to step into bravery. For those who find themselves stuck, alone or without hope, it will surely bring not only helpful encouragement, but also the wonderful feeling that you are not crazy, your struggles are not your identity, and within everyone there is a call to live a life full of bravery."

Christy Wimber, pastor, author and teacher

"This is an honest, heartfelt account about what it really means to be brave. I found it easy to read but also truly impacting. If you're facing huge challenges or everyday struggles, this book is for you. Highly recommended."

Steve Legg, magician, escapologist and editor of *Sorted* magazine

"This is an honest, real and practical book to help us find courage through the seasons of life. Debbie draws on her own and others' powerful experiences of being brave through situations like retirement, illness and grief, always pointing to Jesus and His word as the one true anchor in the storm."

Anne Calver, assistant minister at Stanmore Baptist Church

BRAVE

SHOWING
COURAGE
IN ALL
SEASONS
OF LIFE

Debbie Duncan

MONARCH
BOOKS

Published by Monarch Books
an imprint of
Lion Hudson Limited
Wilkinson House,
Jordan Hill Business Park,
Banbury Road, Oxford,
OX2 8DR, England
Email: monarch@lionhudson.com
www.lionhudson.com/monarch

ISBN 978 0 85721 899 5
e-ISBN 978 0 85721 900 8

First edition 2018

Acknowledgments

Unless otherwise stated, Scripture
quotations are taken from the Holy
Bible, New International Version
Anglicised. Copyright © 1979, 1984,
2011 Biblica, formerly International
Bible Society. Used by permission of
Hodder & Stoughton Ltd, an Hachette
UK company. All rights reserved.
"NIV" is a registered trademark
of Biblica. UK trademark number
1448790.

Scripture quotations taken from *The
Message* copyright © by Eugene H.
Peterson 1993, 1994, 1995, 1996,
2000, 2001, 2002. Used by permission
of NavPress Publishing Group.

Scripture quotations marked ESV are
from The Holy Bible, English Standard
Version® (ESV®) copyright © 2001
by Crossway, a publishing ministry
of Good News Publishers. All rights
reserved.

Scripture quotations marked GNB
are from the Good News Bible
published by the Bible Societies and
HarperCollins Publishers, © American
Bible Society 1994, used with
permission.

The Holy Bible, Living Bible Edition,
copyright © Tyndale House Publishers
1971. All rights reserved.

p. 75 "Warning" from *Selected Poems*
by Jenny Joseph, copyright © 1992
Jenny Joseph. Used by permission.

p. 151 Quotations from "A Time to
Live", copyright © 2017 Wellpark
Productions. Used by permission.

A catalogue record for this book is
available from the British Library

Printed and bound in the UK,
February 2018, LH26

Therefore, my dear brothers and sisters, stand firm. Let nothing move you. Always give yourselves fully to the work of the Lord, because you know that your labour in the Lord is not in vain.

1 Corinthians 15:58

This book is dedicated to every person who gets up each morning and puts one foot in front of another. Sometimes that is all you can do. I want to remind you that you are brave.

For Malcolm, my remarkable husband – you help me to be brave. And Matthew, Benjamin, Anna, Riodhna, and Ellie – I thank God for wonderful family.

I also want to dedicate this book to the Gold Hill family. You have loved us through some hard times. I thank God for you all and I am so grateful that we were able to walk part of this journey together.

CONTENTS

ACKNOWLEDGMENTS

Where do I start? There are so many people that I want to thank.

Thank you to Malcolm, my husband. Next year will be our twenty-fifth wedding anniversary. I am so grateful for that day in May. Thank you for being my closest companion. I have learned so much from you. I love you more than ever.

Thank you to Matthew, Benjamin, Anna, and Riodhna for all your support and encouragement. Thank you too to Ellie, and welcome to the family! Rob, you also get a mention.

I also want to thank Dave Bettie for all his help in editing this book. You are a true gentleman. Thank you Matthew for writing about your experiences in an honest and moving way. Thank you Barbara Graham – you challenge and encourage us through your words. I want to thank Richard Simmons for sharing the story of his grandmother with us. Edwina – thank you, too, for all your help.

I would like to thank the old and new family at Monarch Books at Lion: Simon Cox, Jenny Muscat, Joy Tibbs, Jessica Tinker, and Suzanne Wilson-Higgins. You have been through so much change. I hope this book encourages you. Thank you, too, to those at Essential Christian and the Spring Harvest team. You do a remarkable job!

A huge thank you to those who have walked this journey with me. I want to particularly mention the MAD[1] ladies who I travelled to Uganda with: Alison Ball, Lydia Furze, Sue

Furze, Ann Steel, Ruth Tyrell, Abi Webber, and Ruth Webber. Thank you for your encouragement in the later stages of this book. You made me laugh so much I cried when I needed to. I will never forget the dancing in the rain or the tender care you showed the children of Uganda.

BRAVE

by Anna Grace Duncan

Today I don't feel brave,
In fact, it's hard to even breathe,
My head feels heavy;
And my lungs they ache;
Longing, just to take,
A breath of air which strengthens me,
Or a breath of air which allows me to be,
A step away;
From the fearful,
Girl I am today.

"Be brave!" they cried, each step I took;
As I said my first word,
As I read my first book.
"Be brave!" they smiled as my steps got wider;
But courage felt proud,
And the voices were louder.
What would they think?
Or what would they say?
If I spoke up and acted,
In a brave sort of way.
"Be brave! Be strong! Be courageous and driven!"
The instructions they gave –
For a girl who was hidden.

But what does it mean,
To be as brave as they say?
How do I stop;
The fear blocking my way?

You see – I'm learning,
I can't simply become,
Someone fearless and brave –
Afraid of no one.
As my hope becomes weak,
I stop and I pray –
"Oh God, won't someone take,
My fear away?"

But I missed the point,
Missed the core of the notion,
I saw fear as my battle;
And not my solution.
I had called out to God –
"Take it all away!"

But don't you see?
The One I was asking,
The One I had pleaded –
Is the One who helps me steer,
Through all of my fear.

When I took my first steps,
I was brave.
But that doesn't mean –
I wasn't afraid.

You see, bravery relies on fear.
How can you push past something –
Which isn't even here?

To be brave is to act,
Despite the courage you lack,
To be brave is to fight –
Past the worries inside.
To be brave is to walk –
Past the shadows which block,
The warmth of the sun;
And the comfort of the known.

The answer I was seeking,
Was one in two parts –
You need fear to be brave,
Then you trust with your heart –
In God –
The maker, the Father and Creator.

In the words of a song –
It is God who makes us brave,
He calls us out beyond the shore,
And into the waves,
Into the depths of the water,
Leaving comfort behind –
Then, in the arms of our Father,
Fear becomes blind.

But how do I trust him?
Where do I start?
What if my failure –
Has set me apart?
The words of the Father,
Are true and they say:

"Daughter, stop hiding,
Please don't push me away,

I know all your thoughts,
And my love's here to stay.
The answer you're seeking –
It falls at the cross.
Be brave and come close,
Be brave and listen –
You have been chosen,
An heir to a throne,
Where shame drops like the stones,
Your accusers can't throw."

And now?
We have a choice –
Do we gather together –
Strong in one voice?
As women united and rooted in Him.
As women whose failures and sin,
Lie in the sawdust,
Of an old wooden cross –
And paint the large nails,
Covered in rust.

Today we are brave.
For our Father –
Sent his son to save.
Today we are strong,
As we step into His song –
Of freedom of peace,
Of hope and salvation.
And fear?
It can try,
It can try to contain me –
But My King He is near

And helping me be –
A woman no longer
Afraid of the fear.

INTRODUCTION

I am a film buff – I love going to the cinema and also love the fact that in recent times there have been so many films based on real-life stories. They really encourage, enthral, and challenge us. I have certainly used a lot of hankies on my trips to the flicks. I am so glad that on occasion I can watch certain films in the comfort and seclusion of my own home!

There seems to be a trend just now for films based on real people where the main characters seem to show extraordinary bravery. Many of these films are true stories or based on some measure of historical fact. One example is the 2016 Scorsese film *Silence*, starring Liam Neeson and Andrew Garfield, which tells the story of Christian missionaries who face the ultimate test of their faith in seventeenth-century Japan. Although it is based on a book by Japanese author Shusku Endo it does seem to be historically accurate. Liam Neeson plays the part of Cristovao Ferreira (1580–1650) who was actually a Portuguese Catholic priest and missionary who was tortured for his faith. The priests were so brave. I don't know if I could have gone through what they did.

A couple of years ago I was off work recovering from a period of illness. I flicked through the programmes on TV and came across a 2009 film called *The Courageous Heart of*

Irena Sendler. Sendler was a Roman Catholic social worker and humanitarian who ended up working for the Polish underground in German-occupied Warsaw during World War II. She died in 2008 at the grand age of ninety-eight years old. Working with the underground, Irena rescued 2,500 Jewish children from the Warsaw ghetto by pretending to be a nurse (social workers were not allowed in the ghetto). She rescued the children by issuing them with false identities and smuggling them out to safety in suitcases, sacks, or even coffins, and saved more children than any other person during this war. But in 1943 she was captured by the Nazis and tortured for her actions, enduring broken feet and legs. The Nazis were looking for jars that she had buried in her neighbour's garden; the jars were full of the real names and details of those she had saved. She never gave them up. Latterly she was nominated for a Nobel Peace Prize but lost out to Al Gore. It was only in 1999 that she first came to the public attention after her story was dramatized in a play in New York.

When I watched this film I was stunned. I would like to think that I would try to do as Irena did, but I just don't know. I don't know if I could have been that brave in those circumstances.

Recently I was preparing for yet another funeral of a member of our close family. It had been a tough couple of years marked with the dark stain of death. I got up the day before the funeral and wondered if I could cope with all the grief of the following day. Crazily I had popped to the chemist to colour my hair (as the greys had started to reappear) and stood looking at all the boxes. I felt I could not even make a simple decision. I ended up colouring my hair a deep auburn/red. I did not do it to stand out or because I wanted a change. Red was my new colour because in that shop I knew I had to be brave just like Merida in the 2012 Disney Pixar film *Brave*.

In that film sixteen-year-old Princess Merida lives in the mystical kingdom of DunBroch. She is torn between what is expected of a Scottish princess and following her heart. I did mention crazy, didn't I? Sometimes we have to be intentional – to make a choice and stand by it. At this time I had to be brave; my hair colour was a nod to my Scottish heritage and an outward sign of my inward decision to be dependent on God and be brave. Although I made an intentional decision I did not share this with anyone apart from my husband. He even bought me a Princess Merida doll!

Several months later a member of the congregation came and spoke to me. He had something he wanted to share. He told me that he was to tell me "to keep on being brave". The hairs rose on my arms. I knew God was telling me to be ready for more. Within weeks we had another family death and I was in hospital with an asthma attack, pneumonia, and possible heart failure. I had to be brave as I coped with my emotions and waited for test results. I may no longer have red hair, but I am learning about bravery and courage in the face of everyday circumstances.

Many of us find it hard to step out into the unknown. How can we be brave to take those first steps? We are on a journey that consists of lots of steps. Some of us have to change direction, journeying through unknown lands, heading towards places we have never been before.

I am obviously thinking of another film – actually three. Every good film originates from a book – for instance, *The*

Lord of the Rings by J. R. R. Tolkien. Every Christmas season, for three consecutive years (2001–2003), the Duncan family headed to the cinema to see *The Fellowship of the Rings*, *The Two Towers*, and *The Return of the King*. These fantasy films directed by Peter Jackson share the story of hobbit Frodo Baggins and his friends as they carry out a quest to destroy the one ring, fighting incredible battles. Never did Frodo and his brave friend Sam ever think they would leave the peaceful beauty of the Shire. Bravely they step over the boundary of the Shire into worlds unknown.

Whatever film I watch I am left amazed at the story and leave thinking, "I will be braver." I often feel like that though, don't you? I wish I were braver to speak up, to endure what challenges come my way, or step into something new. We hope we will be brave but often we have no idea how we will behave until we are in the middle of a situation.

This books focuses on the different aspects of our journey, from living with chronic illness, parenthood, or providing care for aging parents. We will look at some of the different challenges we face on this road and ask ourselves, "How can we be brave?" At this point I want to remind you that bravery looks different for each of us. We are all different with different journeys ahead of us. Hopefully this book will encourage you if you are living through any of these seasons just now.

We will also examine why we find change difficult and look at behavioural theories that can help us make decisions. One such theory is the cycle of change outlined in chapter 2; used by the addiction services to help people make life-changing decisions. We will at look how the Bible challenges and helps us to trust God during these times.

In doing my research for this book I asked some friends on Facebook for their comments about this topic. What they said highlighted that not all of these steps are big significant ones, such as coping with an illness or chronic disease or the loss of loved ones. Most of our stories will never be made into films but there are many scenes in our lives where we have had to be brave in quiet ways. For some, it is stepping across the threshold of fear and intimidation; for those more introvert of us it is being brave enough to talk to someone new.[1] Being brave looks different for each one of us.

This book is not just about those extraordinary people who challenge world leaders to liberate a nation like Moses or kill a lion on a snowy day like Benaiah.[2] This book is about bravery in those everyday situations that we meet sometimes on a daily basis. How can you be brave when your world changes on the spin of a pin and you are looking at unemployment or a serious health issue?

COURAGE

Give me a spirit that on life's rough sea
Loves to have his sails fill'd with a lusty wind,
Even till his sailyards tremble, his masts crack,
And his rapt ship run on her side so low

That she drinks water, and her keel ploughs air;
There is no danger to a man that knows
What life and death is - there is no law
Exceeds his knowledge: neither is it lawful
That he should stoop to any other law.

George Chapman (1559–1634)

Prayer

Father,

As we step into this book and reflect on the topic of bravery – speak to us.

Let Your words echo through the hills and valleys of our lives.

Use them to help us make brave choices.

Use them to challenge us when we need to be challenged.

Calm our souls when we need to be still.

Heal any hurt or pain that we are reminded of as we dig deeper.

In Jesus' name.

Amen.

CHAPTER 1

WHAT IS BRAVERY?

The Merriam-Webster dictionary defines brave as "having or showing mental or moral strength to face danger, fear, or difficulty: having or showing courage".[1] Perhaps a stronger definition is from the Cambridge Advanced Learner's Dictionary: "Showing no fear of dangerous or difficult things."[2] Wikipedia defines "brave" as "an adjective for one who possesses courage",[3] and "bravery" as "the human condition to confront fear".[4] The word is thought to have originated in the late fifteenth century from the French word meaning "splendid" or "valiant", conjuring up in my mind a picture of a dashing French nobleman or a d'Artagnan-type musketeer! It is also found in the Italian language where "bravo" means "bold". In addition, it has been suggested that its etymological roots come from the Latin "bravus" or "barbarus", meaning "cut-throat" or "villain". Taken together, these ideas paint a picture of a rash, rough, fierce, fearless person – possibly even someone with a poor moral compass. The word is also close to the Latin word "rabidus" meaning "mad, frenzied, wild".

According to my friend Dave, these ideas are also present in the word "berserk". Berserkers (or berserks) were Norse or Viking warriors, frequently described in the Old Icelandic sagas as fighting in a trance-like fury, a characteristic which later gave rise to our English phrase "to go berserk". These champions would often go into battle without mail-coats. It is perhaps not far wide of the mark to say that we would have to be slightly mad to jump into harm's way.

I'm sure that we all know people whom we consider to be brave. At the time of writing I am by the sea in Northern Ireland – one of my favourite places. The news programme last night recounted the story of a brave young man called Andrew Johnston who dived into the swollen Suile Burn near Lifford to rescue an elderly woman, Loreta McKinlay, from a sinking car. Philip and Loreta McKinlay had been driving home that night and for some unknown reason hit the kerb and careered down the embankment, landing in the river. Philip could not rescue his wife so sought help. Andrew was driving past, saw what was going on, and immediately dived into the river. It took four attempts to free Mrs McKinlay from the back seat. Eventually Philip and Andrew managed to get Loreta out of the water and between them they started CPR until the paramedics arrived. She is now in hospital recovering from her ordeal. Andrew thought nothing of his actions and in fact initially left the scene without telling anyone who he was.

He was eventually located and, when asked about the incident, Andrew replied, "What I saw unfolding before me was the scariest thing I have seen in my life."[5] He still leapt into action despite the fear and anxiety he experienced. He left the scene to head to his hotel to change his clothes. It was not until a TV report during the day issued a request for him to come forward that he realized he should identify himself.

He was more concerned, however, about what had happened to Mr and Mrs McKinlay. "I don't want to describe myself as a hero," he said. "I just wanted to find out how the couple were. I'm hoping they will be OK."

Another example of this type of bravery occurred in the city of Cork in 2016 when a female pedestrian was hailed as a hero having dramatically rescued a three-year-old child who had slipped and fallen into the Lee.[6] She too knew that she had to save the child and acted on her instinct.

After the bombing at the Ariana Grande concert in Manchester in 2017, there were countless reports of brave and heroic people. One example was that of Lianna Shutt, a mother and former nurse. She saved a stranger who was bleeding to death by driving him from the scene of the bomb blast to hospital at 100 mph.[7] Lianna's own daughter was at the Manchester Arena when the bomb went off, and was protected from the impact of the blast by a stranger. Even Ariana Grande's mother, Joan Grande, helped panicked young fans backstage to safety after the explosion at the singer's concert.

If we scour the press we will find hundreds of these stories of everyday men, women, or children who do not consider themselves a hero or to be particularly brave. These are people who see a need and jump into rivers or shield a child from harm. What qualities do they have to enable them to become unassuming heroes? We call them brave but what do we mean by this?

In art and literature there are so many heroes, from Disney's Merida of DunBroch to Samwise Gamgee in J. R. R. Tolkien's *The Lord of the Rings*. In terms of imagery we think of the brave and ferocious king of the animals, the lion. In the famous Chronicles of Narnia series by C. S. Lewis the main character Aslan is very brave, displaying both strength and humility. Author and artist Mary Anne Radmacher once wrote: "Courage doesn't always roar. Sometimes courage is the little voice at the end of the day that says 'I'll try again tomorrow.'"[8] As we shall see, bravery is not always embodied as a lion, however.

Or how about this? In 2017 the former US President George W. Bush published a book of paintings to commemorate some of the veterans he had met since leaving office in 2009. It is called *Portraits of Courage: A Commander in Chief's Tribute to America's Warriors* and contains sixty-six full-colour portraits of physically and/or mentally traumatized US Armed Forces veterans of the Afghanistan and Iraq wars and depicts images of bravery.

Bravery in the Bible

When I think of biblical characters who were known for their bravery I think of the shepherd boy David protecting his sheep against bandits, wolves, and even mountain lions. I think of a weak, fearful Moses who hated speaking out publicly, let alone leading a nation. When God asked him to lead the Israelite slaves to freedom Moses had five excuses not to lead them. He told God: "I'm not good enough"; "I don't have the answers"; "the people won't believe I heard from You"; "I am not a public speaker"; and "I'm not even qualified to lead." He finally said: "Anyone but me." Yet within a few chapters of Exodus he had spoken to the Israelites, confronted Pharaoh, and led a nation to freedom.

I also think of Deborah, the only female judge mentioned in the Bible: she was a prophetess and ruled with wisdom during a time when the role of women was so different to how it is today. Israel was oppressed by King Jabin of Canaan for about twenty years. Deborah heard from God and told Barak to muster his troops and fight Sisera, Jabin's army commander, because God would be with him. Barak refused to fight without the presence of Deborah and the people recognized that the battle was won by a woman. She went on to reign as judge for over forty years, during which time there was peace in the land. As a politico-judicial authority she was also called "a mother in Israel".

In Matthew 14:28–31 Jesus beckoned Peter to step out of the boat and to walk towards him across the Sea of Galilee, which is estimated to be 140–200 feet deep. There was a violent storm raging, possibly caused by the cool air from the mountains meeting the lake basin in the Jordan Rift, or fierce winds hitting from the Golan Heights. The funnelling winds can cause waves to reach nearly ten foot high. Wouldn't you be afraid?

I think Peter needs to be praised for stepping out of the fishing boat into the waters of the Lake of Galilee. Jesus may have needed to rescue him but it was this experienced fisherman who got out of the safe boat into the wild seas. He took the initial step.

We have lots of these challenges though, don't we? Some of us may feel we are not brave enough to step into new challenges. We are so frightened about changing the status quo that we may miss the blessing that come with stepping out. One of my children struggles with change. I am sure part of his problem is due to our having moved so much when he was young. We counted it up one day and I think we moved about nineteen times since we got married. My mum is fed up with having to keep updating her address book.

But back to the story. When results day came for his A levels our son was disappointed. He had lined up a job in the care sector and would not consider university clearing. Through an amazing turn of events, by the end of the day, he had a place to study his chosen topic and had to move within the week. We were all in shock. In an amazing way he was pushed out of the boat.

There are so many other brave characters in the Bible. Take Ruth, for example, whose story we read in the Old Testament book named after her. Ruth was married to her husband for about ten years when he and his brother both died, leaving Ruth to care for her widowed mother-in-law. Orpah, her sister-in-law, returned home to her own people but Ruth insisted on staying with Naomi: "But Ruth replied, 'Don't urge me to leave you or to turn back from you. Where you go I will go, and where you stay I will stay. Your people will be my people and your God my God'" (Ruth1:16).

Ruth went with her mother-in-law, Naomi, to a foreign land; Esther spoke up for her people; and Daniel refused to deny the God he served. We have already heard of Benaiah, one of David's mighty men, who had to be brave when stranded in a pit on a snowy day – with a lion! There are so many others we can learn from. They found themselves in situations that required them to have courage and to be brave for a season.

There is the prostitute Rahab, who hid the Israelite spies in Jericho and whose entire family was spared by her actions.

And then there is Mary, a teenager and unmarried mother-to-be who could have been stoned for carrying a child. How were people to know she was carrying God's child? They probably thought she had had sex before marriage – an offence punishable by stoning.

I think we can all recount stories of bravery or describe what it looks like. It's the soldier off to war, the hero who saved someone from drowning, the child living with cancer, a friend battling with depression, our children going to a new school. We have all had to make decisions to act in the face of fear, to have courage, and be brave. We often use the words bravery and courage to describe the same event. They appear to mean the same thing but I do think there is a difference between them.

What is courage?

Courage is often considered as the mental or moral strength or ability that enables a person to try something new, to venture out into the unknown, and to persevere or withstand danger or fear. Courage involves mindfulness or a level of emotional intelligence. There is often a cause, such as love or compassion.

Courage is said to come from the French word "coeur" which means "heart". Others take it back even further to the Latin "cor" or "heart". Either way we can agree with the American scholar, author, and research professor Brené Brown who calls courage a "heart word" as it reflects the heart's inner strength. Being courageous therefore involves facing our fears with heart and mind. In fact, in Brené Brown's most popular TEDx (technology, entertainment and design) talk of all time (over 32 million people have viewed it online) she suggests that to live a full life requires courage as we often have to do things that make us feel vulnerable and even afraid.[9]

So where does the concept of courage come from? In philosophy we can trace it back to Plato who lived from 428 to 348 BC. He wrote about this particular subject, including many definitions, but did not himself come to a definitive conclusion about it. In his early dialogue *Laches* Plato had this to say: "[courage is]… a sort of endurance of the soul…", "[courage is]… knowledge of the grounds of fear". In his later work *The Republic*, Plato tried to describe courage as being perseverance through emotions such as suffering, pleasure, and fear.[10]

In early Christian faith courage is considered to be the same as fortitude, being held to be one of the seven gifts of the Holy Spirit. Thomas Aquinas also believed that courage was a virtue, particularly when used with love, mercy, and conviction. He defined fortitude or courage as the removal of "any obstacle that keeps the will from following reason".[11] Augustine, on the other hand, identified courage in those who do not have faith and did not consider it a Christian virtue. David Hume, the seventeenth-century Scottish philosopher, defined courage as a natural virtue found in all humanity. In the Eastern traditions, courage is believed to be derived from love, and in Islam courage and self-control are strongly linked.

Paul Tillich was a German American who is widely regarded as one of the most influential theologians of the twentieth century. He equated courage with religion, defining it as "the self-affirmation of being in spite of the fact of non-being".

Courage is a virtue rightly celebrated across the spectrum of humanity. Sir Winston Churchill once said, "Courage is rightly esteemed the first of human qualities because it is the quality that guarantees all others." As a Christian, I would suggest that love is the most important of human virtues and it is from love that courage is birthed. It is right to celebrate it in all people but we also know that it can deepen and become so much more vibrant when allowed to grow through God's Spirit in us.

Courage in the Bible

In the Bible bravery and courage are viewed as attributes associated with knowing that God is present and with following His will. Joshua 1:9 says, "Have I not commanded you? Be strong and courageous. Do not be frightened, and do not be dismayed, for the Lord your God is with you wherever you go" (ESV). In 1 Chronicles 28:20 (ESV) David says to his son Solomon: "Be strong and courageous and do it. Do not be afraid and do not be dismayed, for the Lord God, even my God, is with you. He will not leave you or forsake you."

I think of Gideon, a fearful man who hid in a winepress and then became a mighty leader. Gideon[12] lived during a dark time in Israel's history (we are unsure when he was born but he probably lived between 1380 and 1050 BC when there was a struggle for power and leadership as the country's old enemies began to resurface. Israel did not put God first and allowed themselves to be ruled by their own hearts. Oppressive tribal groups such as the Midianites, Amalekites, and other groups from the East would attack Israel during their harvest time, destroying their crops and pillaging the land. Gideon was hiding out, threshing wheat in a winepress of all places because he was too afraid to be threshing the wheat outside. God spoke to Gideon, foreseeing the kind of man he could become. He spoke into Gideon's life, reminding him of the God he served and that he was not alone. He was encouraged to be courageous and brave during a season when Israel needed a brave new leader. He then stepped out with courage.

In the New Testament the Greek word that is translated as "courage" literally means "boldness and confidence". Courage is considered to be the opposite of fear. In our society courage and bravery are generally considered to be synonyms although in philosophy they differ in meaning as courage involves the presence of fear, while bravery suggests the absence of fear. In a *HuffPost* article called, "What Is the Difference between Bravery and Courage?", Ronit Avni, the Peabody Award-winning media producer, writes about the Israeli-Palestinian conflict in Gaza. She suggests that courage is more sustainable and a longer-term solution than acts of bravery. She hints that courage mixed with vision will create long-term change in the area.

I understand what she is saying but I disagree. The Scottish politician Alex Salmond once said: "In various times in history ordinary people can make a difference." I believe that bravery is courage for a season. There are specific times when we need to be brave. Who can have courage all the time unless we are fully aware we are in God's presence? Only God and His perfect love can redeem fear and fill our hearts with courage. Being courageous is not something we can do on our own. It is a quality that is enriched by God as we learn that we can trust Him and not be afraid. It is a quality we need for specific seasons in our lives.

Courage therefore is to brave as breathing is to life, as intellect is to thinking, as sight is to vision. Courage helps us to be brave in a period of time when we have to be fearless. In John 16:33 Jesus said: "I have told you these things, so that in me you may have peace. In this world you will have trouble. But take heart! I have overcome the world."

Prayer

Father God,

Thank you that Your perfect love casts out fear. We can come to know that love through the life, death, and resurrection of Your Son, Jesus.

Thank you that You do not leave us alone but that You want a relationship with us that gives us a purpose and a hope. You remind us to take courage because one day You will return and there will be an end to all pain and suffering.

Thank you, in Jesus' name.

Amen.

CHAPTER 2

COPING WITH CHANGE

I have met a lot of people whose biggest challenge has been coping with change. They have had to show immense bravery as they adapt to changes in their lives. In this chapter we are going to look at some of the big changes throughout history. We will consider what might happen when people don't cope with change, theories of change, and also look at what the Bible teaches us about this topic. Are there ways we can adapt to the changes in our lives with a brave spirit?

Were you told while you were growing up that people believed the "flat earth" myth until the Middle Ages? In actual fact, even the early Greeks believed the earth was spherical,[1] and not many people believed it wasn't round at all. Stephen Gould argues that the flat-earth theory came to prominence between 1870 and 1920 as people struggled with more modern thinking about evolution. In the face of such huge theoretical challenges, it is no wonder that people returned to the old ways of thinking. I used to wonder what people thought when it was first proved that the world was round not flat. How many people had only travelled as far as their horizon because they were scared they would fall off the end of the world? Did they plan an adventure to go beyond what they could see or did they stay put? Sometimes we cannot see what is ahead of us if it involves change, and that is one area where we have to be brave – brave enough to step into unknown territory.

Did you know that the American standard railway gauge is four feet, eight-and-one-half inches? It is an odd measurement, isn't it? The reason why the space between the two rails was this distance was because they were following the British model, and American railways were built by British expatriates. When the railways were first built in the US the public were fearful that they would be the downfall of the nation!

This is part of a letter to President Jackson dated 31 January 1829:

> As you may know, Mr. President, "railroad" carriages are pulled at the enormous speed of 15 miles per hour by "engines" which, in addition to endangering life and limb of passengers, roar and snort their way through the countryside, setting fire to crops, scaring the livestock and frightening women and children. The Almighty certainly never intended that people should travel at such breakneck speed.

Martin Van Buren, Governor of New York

The train example is perhaps easy to understand but what about the potato? There are over 200 varieties of potato. In fact, 99 per cent of them originate from the country of Chile. In Britain supermarkets sell at least sixteen types of chips[2] and 87 per cent of us love them.[3] It is hard to believe now, but the potato was originally a really unpopular food. When potatoes were first introduced into England by Sir Walter Raleigh, newspapers printed less than favourable editorials about them, ministers preached sermons against this new dietary trend, and the general public did not take to them. It soon became the answer to famine among the poorer classes but it was years before the nobility embraced the idea of having mashed, chipped, fried, and roasted or jacket potatoes after all the adverse publicity.[4]

There are so many food products that are now common items on the supermarket shelves. Look at pasta. Pasta has now topped a global survey of the world's favourite foods. We have probably all had spaghetti bolognese, lasagne, or carbonara, but pasta did not become a staple of the British diet until the 1960s. In 1987 pasta sales in the UK were worth £53 million; in 2009 this had increased to £292 million.[5]

I think we have lived in a time of some of the biggest changes in history. In the eleventh century the biggest change to society was the building of castles. In the thirteenth century it was the establishment of the marketplace. The twentieth century's biggest change was the Russian Revolution. In 1900 most people did not have a phone. Even as late as the 1960s people had to use payphones to contact people. By 2000 approximately 40 per cent of us had a mobile phone! Do you remember the brick-sized mobile phones of the 1980s or the laughable concept that you could have a visual image of people using a tele communicator on *Star Trek*? I remember laughing with my mum about the fact there would one day be communicators that would have a visual display, where people could ring and see what you were doing while being on the phone.

Do you remember the BBC programme *Tomorrow's World*? In 1967 they looked at the idea of having a home computer. In a later episode they looked at mobile phones. As a child I was amazed by some of the inventions on the programme. Nowadays a lot of the products they showed us then have become a part of my everyday life. Who would have predicted in the 1960s that the technology used in Apollo 11, the first spaceflight that landed the first two humans on the moon, had less technology than is present in your mobile phone today? Ian Mortimer's article in *The Guardian* in 2014 reports: "Today we predict almost everything: what the weather will be, what housing we will need, what our pensions will be worth, where we will dispose of our rubbish for the next 30 years and so on."[6]

We are also aware that there are so many changes happening in our world. Almost twenty-five years ago, at a meeting in Cairo coordinated by the United Nations, the international community gathered to explore how the world was changing and how those changes were affecting the most vulnerable. At the International Conference on Population and Development (ICPD), the world agreed that there were significant population challenges around such persistent issues as family planning, maternal and child health, migration, and gender equality. One current example is the European refugee crisis, which started in early 2015 and has become the largest refugee crisis since World War II. In 2015 more than a million people fled from the fighting in Syria, Afghanistan, and Iraq. World dynamics are changing rapidly – after all, who would have ever predicted ten years ago that Donald Trump would be the president of the United States or that Britain would have voted to leave the European Union?

So how do we change with these seismic shifts in the landscapes of our world? What do you do when you have been working in the same job for fifteen years and are made redundant or your children leave home to head to university? Psychologists call this "transition". A transition is the shift from a period of familiar-and-known to a different place. Each transition involves the end of the current and present and moving to something new. Each of us has to cope with change. Each major change, like going to a new school, starting a new job, or the end of a relationship comes with its own share of stress. Even the most flexible or resilient of people can feel anxious or stressed.

When things go wrong

Sometimes the feelings of stress and anxiety can persist for several months and can lead to an adjustment disorder. It is a temporary condition caused by stress and linked with psychological and physical symptoms that can interfere with everyday life. With an adjustment disorder people experience a more severe reaction than would normally be expected. Such a response may be to one event or several events such as marital or financial problems. Symptoms can vary from depressed mood, anxiety, or disturbance of conduct to maladaptive reactions.[7] Adjustment disorders are commonly treated with psychotherapy, medication, or a combination of both. It is therefore important that we do all we can to prevent such reactions and one way to do this is to increase our resilience to overcome stressors.

There are many ways to increase resilience and I have outlined these in my previous book, *The Art of Daily Resilience*.[8]

The following are just a few simple suggestions:

- develop a strong network of people to support you

- live healthily, caring for body, soul, and mind

- establish a good understanding of who you are in Christ

- utilize the theories of change that help us understand what change is and develop strategies that help us cope with it.

Theories of change

There are various strategies about change that we can adapt and use. Most theories about how we cope are written for organizations, but I believe we can use them at a more personal level. The five-step approach suggests that the following strategies are required to navigate change within an organization:[9]

1. Be clear about the purpose for the change. I would suggest that we need to be realistic and honest about what is happening.

2. Understand and communicate the complexity of the change needed. Communication is important. That includes communication between you and God and your family, friends, and church.

3. Take the necessary time to help people understand why change is needed now. On a personal basis, take time to understand why this change has to happen. Consider any resistance you have in your own life.

4. Explore the reasons behind any resistance you experience to change. Sometimes you simply have to be brave.

5. Use internal facilitators to ensure that the change process taps into the strengths of what you are trying to change, whether it is an institution or yourself. I would suggest that as part of a fellowship you can ask others to help you work it out. There is a Quaker discipline sometimes called the Council of Discernment. It goes something like this: when you are facing significant change in life, ask a few wise friends to sit with you. They will listen as you explain the circumstances around the change. The council members do not offer commentary but only ask clarifying questions as light shining into a situation. We can ask God to do that through the body of His church and the leading of His Spirit.[10]

The theory of change is at its heart a comprehensive description and illustration of how and why a desired change is expected to happen in a particular context. It is focused on the gap between the implementation and the desired goals. The theory of change also defines long-term goals and then maps backwards to identify necessary preconditions.[11] It cannot be viewed as a linear model because human beings are organic and dynamic. Behaviour and change are often circular. An example of this is the five stages of grief model by Kübler-Ross.[12]

Originally Kübler-Ross' model was considered as a stages model in which a person goes through one stage at a time. In reality, grief is more like a bowl of spaghetti – we experience the different stages at different times; there is no set pattern for us all. We all process things differently and it is the same with change.

The theory of change is often also considered as a process model which leads theory into action and includes monitoring and evaluation, adjustment of the theory and implementation, and so on. In essence we have a strategy to implement and help us cope with change, and if it doesn't work we look at another plan.

I remember when our first son went to university. He was coping with the change of leaving home and heading to Keele University. He was offered his place just a week before he went. Malcolm and I were left with a huge gaping Matthew-shaped hole when he set off. I spent the week running around getting him organized and not thinking about him leaving home. My plan to help me cope with change was to organize things. (My family tell me I do that a lot.) Once we dropped Matthew off at university I could not do that any more. We cried all the way home from taking him to university. I could not go into his bedroom at home for about a month after he left. I needed another strategy. What happened was that God reminded me that this was His plan for Matthew and his life. I was able to cope with the change in family life as God gave me the courage for the season – I was able to be brave.

Behavioural change

Sometimes change is not about an event we are coping with but the change that needs to happen in our own life. This is easy for me as I know there are so many areas that need to change. One of the simple yet lifelong areas that I have had to let God change in me is simply to say "sorry" when things go wrong. So often in the past I have tried to over-analyse an event when all I simply had to do is say "sorry". I am not exactly sure why I do it but I have my theories!

Scripture teaches that God's plan for us is the transformation of our character so we become more like Jesus.[13] No one is perfect; we are all flawed. If we have asked Christ into our hearts we are under His grace. It is His grace that frees us and changes us. He also promises us that He will guide us and that He is with us.[14] The journey is not one we have to make by ourselves. The breath of His Spirit blows into the sails of our lives. None of us can change without God's help. Paul appealed to the church in Rome: "Do not conform to the pattern of this world, but be transformed by the renewing of your mind. Then you will be able to test and approve what God's will is – his good, pleasing and perfect will" (Romans 12:2).

Paul also wrote: "I have been crucified with Christ and I no longer live, but Christ lives in me. The life I now live in the body, I live by faith in the Son of God, who loved me and gave himself for me" (Galatians 2:20).

Psychology teaches us that there are cycles or stages to the process of change. Prochaska and DiClemente's model (2005) outlines a variety of stages a person goes through when changing behaviour.[15] It is often used by the addiction services and in smoking cessation. The stages are as follows.

Precontemplation: There is often no intention of changing behaviour and the person may be unaware that a problem exists. This may be the point they are challenged about it. I would suggest that as a Christian we should constantly be aware that we need to change and become more like Jesus.

Contemplation: At this stage the person becomes aware that there is a problem but has not committed to change. If we are in tune with God's Spirit and dependent on His word we will be aware that we do not live the life we should. I am reminded of what the apostle Paul says in Romans 7:15–20:

> I do not understand what I do. For what I want to do
> I do not do, but what I hate I do. And if I do what I
> do not want to do, I agree that the law is good. As it
> is, it is no longer I myself who do it, but it is sin living
> in me. For I know that good itself does not dwell in
> me, that is, in my sinful nature. For I have the desire
> to do what is good, but I cannot carry it out. For I do
> not do the good I want to do, but the evil I do not
> want to do – this I keep on doing. Now if I do what
> I do not want to do, it is no longer I who do it, but it
> is sin living in me that does it.

It is also a good time to be able to seek advice and wisdom from an accountability group.

Preparation: The person is intentional about making the change. In the model this may involve an increased self-efficacy where the client believes s/he can make change. When approaching it from a faith perspective I would suggest that the client is more aware they need God's help. As in the contemplation stage, spending time in God's presence will always lead us to want to change.

Action: The person is actively changing their behaviour. This speaks for itself.

Maintenance: During this phase sustained change occurs and new behaviours replace the old ones.

Relapse: Often the person falls back into old patterns of behaviour. I do know that God is forgiving and patient with me. I still don't always say sorry but I am a work in progress.

Precontemplation: And back to the start. The person may be unaware that there's a problem, thus there is no intention to change their behaviour.

The amazing thing about God is that when we journey with Him He takes us at the speed we need to be at. He can take us through these stages at a comfortable walking pace of two miles an hour or we may race through it at sixty miles an hour. He is our Creator God and has the ability to enable His Spirit to move us through these stages as He will.

Change in the Bible

I think what has helped me is God reminding me that He **does not** change. It is good to remind ourselves of the nature of God. God is not only eternal, omnipresent, and present in every moment; in Malachi 3:6 God told the Israelites: "I am the Lord, and I do not change. And so you, the descendants of Jacob, are not yet completely lost" (GNT). In the New Testament Jesus reminded us that He and the Father are one. Hebrews 13:8 says, "Jesus Christ is the same yesterday, today, and forever" (GNT). This is encouraging because there is a trend in theology called process theology, or panentheism, where individuals believe that God is evolving or ever changing. Our God does not change; His attributes do not change.

Read Malachi 3:6 again. As Christians we sometimes need to remind ourselves that change can be constructive and helpful in our spiritual transformation.

In the Forsa Church in Hälsingland in Sweden there is a triptych from the beginning of the sixteenth century. It is a painting of the church as a ship. The mast of the ship is the cross of Christ, which supports the sails. The passengers are old patriarchs and bishops. The ship is on a journey, called by the triune God, to take part in the mission of God in the world. The challenge for us is that when there is a storm we want to be anchored in the harbour. We want to stay in our safe place. We want the status quo. Often we grow better when we are stretched, during times of adversity or when God uproots us physically or spiritually for our own good. God may not have caused the difficulties we are in but He can certainly use them for our good.[16]

What I am saying is: change can be good for us.

God never changes, but as Christians we should not stay as we are.

We can be brave and adapt and cope with change if we trust God.

God has sent His Spirit to help us become more like Jesus.

One of the most famous photos of the Earth was taken in 1972 by the Apollo 17 crew, consisting of astronaut Eugene A. Cernan, commander; astronaut Ronald E. Evans, command module pilot; and scientist-astronaut Harrison H. Schmitt, lunar module pilot. The translunar coast photograph shows the Earth from the Mediterranean Sea area to the Antarctic polar ice cap. It is known as the "Blue Marble" and was the first time people really saw what their whole planet looked like from space. The concept of the Earth had changed from being flat, to a sphere to a beautiful blue marble. Throughout these changes people had to be brave and accept them.

Whether you are eating potatoes – diced, cubed, chipped, or even roasted – for the first time, or taking a journey at a speed you are not used to, you can be brave. God enables us to have the courage for the things we cannot change and for the changes that we face in our everyday lives.

Prayer

Father,

Thank you for reminding us that You never change. You are the Alpha and Omega – the beginning and the end. Even when life is rocky and full of changes You remind us You are the same – we can trust in You. You can also use the events in our lives for good.

Thank you that we don't do this alone.

In Jesus' name.

Amen.

CHAPTER 3

BRAVERY IN THE FACE
OF ILL HEALTH

I think it is ironic that as I write this I am recovering from another bout of illness. For two days it looked unlikely that I would be able to go on a short-term trip to Uganda. People in church were telling me how brave they thought I was, trying to go even though I have a chronic illness. I do not feel brave. Certainly when I am ill I feel most vulnerable and definitely not brave. I want to go as I believe that God can use me and also change me.

Lisa Copen is an American speaker and writer committed to raising awareness around the impact of chronic illness or long-term conditions. In a *Huffpost* blog dating from 2010, Copen asked: "Why are we expected to be brave in the face of illness?"[1] Her posting discussed the media response to celebrities such as Michael Douglas and his battle with cancer or Jean-Claude Van Damme, the Belgian actor, and his recovery from a heart attack. Copen's point was that there are so many people who never get a mention in the press who face the battle with chronic illness on a daily basis, and yet are not acknowledged as being brave. It is a really interesting question and one we can also ask of ourselves in our faith communities where so many people live remarkable lives and have to be brave through a season of chronic illness.

In the UK it is reported that more than 15 million people live with a long-term condition.[2] According to Department of Health statistics (2012), this equates to 58 per cent of people over sixty and prevalence is even higher in people in the poorest social classes.[3] We also know that these figures are on the increase because many long-term conditions such as type 2 diabetes, hypertension (persistent high blood pressure), or obstructive respiratory diseases are under-diagnosed. The picture is further compounded by an inexorably aging population with complex long-term needs, and not simply those of a physical nature.

Mental health problems are a growing public health issue in the UK and the rest of the world. Some have suggested that mental health problems such as anxiety, depression, or behavioural issues are the main cause of disability in people aged twenty to twenty-nine.[4] Physical health and mental health are known to be interlinked. As whole people we consist of body, soul, and mind. Anxiety is the second biggest cause of illness worldwide. It is the main trigger of both suicide and cardiovascular disease. One in four people in the UK is said to experience a significant mental illness in their adult lifetime and that figure is thought to be underestimated – with some researchers suggesting that it may be as high as one in three.[5] The shame and stigma of mental illness are gradually being broken down, and campaigns spearheaded by prominent individuals, including Princes William and Harry, have done much to shift the spotlight onto this area.

It is therefore amazing to think that despite the prevalence of mental illness, considerable stigma still attaches to it, not just in our communities but also in our churches.[6]

I want to shout this out so that there can be no misunderstandings about what I am going to say: *people with long-term physical and/or mental illness are brave!* Can you imagine living a life when you constantly have to monitor the food you eat or take twice as long as anyone else to walk to the shops? It is so hard to walk a mile in someone's shoes. You do not know what challenges people have unless you ask them.

I love this poem by Emm Roy. It is called "Mental Illness".

> People assume you aren't sick
> unless they see the sickness on your skin
> like scars forming a map of all the ways you're hurting.
>
> My heart is a prison of Have you tried?
> Have you tried exercising? Have you tried eating better?
> Have you tried not being sad, not being sick?
> Have you tried being more like me?
> Have you tried shutting up?
>
> Yes, I have tried. Yes, I am still trying,
> and yes, I am still sick.
>
> Sometimes monsters are invisible, and
> sometimes demons attack you from the inside.
> Just because you cannot see the claws and the teeth
> does not mean they aren't ripping through me.
> Pain does not need to be seen to be felt.

*Telling me there is no problem
won't solve the problem.*

*This is not how miracles are born.
This is not how sickness works.*[7]

As a nurse, lecturer, and pastor's wife I have met so many people who fit this description. I like to remind my patients that they are brave. They exhibit courage in the face of devastating news or gruelling treatment. Imagine having to have blood tests every couple of days for six months – especially if you have a needle phobia – or receiving treatment that means you lose your hair, youthful appearance, and ability to conceive and you are so fatigued and sick that you can't stand up. Or you may have to monitor everything you eat, have daily injections, take oral medication, and your life is structured around clinic and doctors' appointments. Or perhaps you have escalating levels of anxiety and depression that make you want to end your life or you have not left your home for more than eight years. I can think of hundreds of names as I write these sentences.

I am a lecturer in nursing and a respiratory specialist nurse. I often have to teach my students about what patients experience as they live with a chronic respiratory disease. The American actor Steve Martin once said: "Before you criticize a man, walk a mile in his shoes. That way, when you do criticize him, you'll be a mile away and have his shoes."

Putting the humour to one side, I sometimes teach my students breathing techniques so that they can identify with their patients and so gain some insight into what it feels like to be breathless. Have you ever thought about what it means to be so out of breath that you cannot walk to your kitchen to make a cup of tea without stopping to rest and catch your breath? It is a horrible sensation that I know well from personal experience. I have a chronic respiratory condition caused by brittle asthma and having had methicillin-resistant Staphylococcus aureus (MRSA) in my lungs. (MRSA is one of those really nasty superbugs that is resistant to mainstream antibiotics.) Every now and then I develop pneumonia that leaves me with persistent breathlessness for four to six weeks. Simply having a shower can take an hour. I would not want anyone to feel the way it makes me feel. Sometimes every breath is a challenge but I know that there are hundreds and thousands of people who live with greater challenges than I do. I don't know what everyday life is like for them so I asked people on my Facebook page about their experience of living with a long-term condition. One lady replied: "You wake up every day with the same difficulties in front of you and they will probably get worse the older you become. Being brave is to wake up saying I will PRAISE the Lord, I will REJOICE in God my Saviour, I will give THANKS." What a challenge!

Choose your words wisely

So what can we do to help? The first thing I want to say is: *choose your words wisely.* Former lecturer in biblical theology and now a writer, campaigner, and broadcaster, Tanya Marlow describes her struggle with long-term illness in *Premier Christianity* magazine: "As someone who has had a chronic illness for 21 years, I've heard my fair share of inappropriate and insensitive advice and comments, including from well-meaning Christians."[8] She goes on to list five ways we can support people with Myalgic Encephalomyelitis (ME), the first being to listen, and believe. Often as we seek to help people, we speak inappropriate words that become like arrows to the heart. Listen to their story and don't try and fix them.

We also have to be careful not to reflect our theology of health and wellness on those who are journeying with chronic illness. We may believe we all have the right to be healed. We have to be careful not to reflect our theology on the person who has a daily battle with illness. I absolutely believe that God heals; I know He heals but these are acts of grace. There are people who have prayed for healing all their lives and not been healed.

When I was at university I met Eileen,[9] a lady who had been a wheelchair user since having had a terrible accident as a teenager. She attended a church meeting where a man prophesied that she would one day be able to dance in her dancing shoes. She confided to me that so many people had told her she would be healed. She took me through to her bedroom and showed me her chest of drawers. Every drawer was filled with pairs of stockings – there must have been hundreds of them. She was living on the breadline and could not afford to buy things she would never wear, yet each pair of stockings was a physical sign of hope. Eileen died without ever wearing her stockings and dancing shoes although I know she is now twirling to the beat of Heaven. *We have to be very careful not to reflect our theology on people.*

Try not to label people

Another lady called Mary explained that she had developed epilepsy (petit mal) and she found that people had become afraid of her. She went on to explain that she felt people had labelled her as an epileptic rather than seeing her as a person who happens to have epilepsy or an impediment. Mary told me that she is now used to the label and understands that other people are the ones with the impediment in their thinking. Despite this, Mary knows that in her spirit she has no impediment and that is the part which matters the most: the rest is just physical. Bravery comes in all shapes and sizes, and Mary is one example of this.

We need to remind ourselves that a long-term condition, illness, or disability is never an impediment in God's eyes. He sees who we truly are. We have no labels with God. An illness or disability impacts our physical being but not our spirits. Bravery is seen when we seek that direct connection with God, no matter how bad things get in a "human" sense. In our church communities we have to be careful not to home in on a person's disability first. We are all made in God's image.

A number of years ago I was in Nepal with a team from the International Nepal Fellowship (INF) visiting the Green Pastures Hospital in Pokhara, a hospital opened in 1957 to support people suffering from leprosy. The staff there now focus on treatment and rehabilitation for people living with spinal cord injuries and other physical disabilities. It provides support to thousands of people and has earned a reputation for delivering a high standard of care to the poorest and most marginalized people of Nepal.[10] I was asked to speak at their weekly patient devotions and shared the story of Mephibosheth.

According to the second book of Samuel in the Old Testament, Mephibosheth (whose name means "from the mouth of shame") was the son of Jonathan and grandson of King Saul. When he was five years old both his father and grandfather died at the Battle of Mount Gilboa. Mephibosheth's nurse took him and fled in panic but in her haste she dropped him and he was unable to walk again. Some years later, when David became king of the united kingdom of Israel, he sought out "someone of the house of Saul, to whom I may show the kindness of God". At that point they remembered Mephibosheth but thought that David would not want to see him because he was a "cripple". Mephibosheth actually referred to himself as a "dead dog". David brought him to the king's table, restored Saul's inheritance to Mephibosheth and allowed him to live within his palace in Jerusalem. David knew Mephibosheth's birthright. He did not see him as disabled, but like a son; the son of a king.

I shared these words in the hospital in Pokhara with people who had been ravaged by leprosy or had spinal cord defects. They had been rejected by society. I was able to tell them that God welcomes them to His table, and that He provides for them at a place of green pastures. Those moments were so special – I could almost touch the Spirit of God resting on their lives and watched as these bowed-down people realized that God accepted them as they were.

Here is Mephibosheth's story as recounted in 2 Samuel 9:6–13:

> When Mephibosheth son of Jonathan, the son of Saul, came to David, he bowed down to pay him honour.

David said, "Mephibosheth!"

"At your service," he replied.

"Don't be afraid," David said to him, "for I will surely show you kindness for the sake of your father Jonathan. I will restore to you all the land that belonged to your grandfather Saul, and you will always eat at my table."

Mephibosheth bowed down and said, "What is your servant, that you should notice a dead dog like me?"

Then the king summoned Ziba, Saul's steward, and said to him, "I have given your master's grandson everything that belonged to Saul and his family. You and your sons and your servants are to farm the land for him and bring in the crops, so that your master's grandson may be provided for. And Mephibosheth, grandson of your master, will always eat at my table." (Now Ziba had fifteen sons and twenty servants.)

Then Ziba said to the king, "Your servant will do whatever my lord the king commands his servant to do." So Mephibosheth ate at David's table like one of the king's sons.

Mephibosheth had a young son named Mika, and all the members of Ziba's household were servants of Mephibosheth. And Mephibosheth lived in Jerusalem, because he always ate at the king's table; he was lame in both feet.

Some of the bravest people I know don't always look like we do. They don't always communicate like we do. They don't always act like we do. God sees them as His children, no different from you or me. *We need to learn to see people as God does.*

Ask directly how you can help

In general, people may not need help but perhaps there are times when life becomes a little more challenging. A lady in our church family approached me a few years ago and basically told me to phone her anytime I needed a meal cooked for the family. She knew I was working and generally managed but there are times when life is a little tougher than usual. She has been a blessing on a number of occasions.

I am a part of the Pentecostal arm of the church. While it is beautiful, diverse and breathtaking, it can, however, have its challenges. We have a strong theology of healing but are not so robust in our thinking when we consider a theology of suffering. Although we can give a Christian answer which is more intellectually satisfying than that offered by other religions, we still live with the dichotomy between healing and suffering. Perhaps this is because in Western cultures suffering has been seen as being bad or something to be avoided. Certainly, in most parts of the world, the church is familiar with adversity. Living in the prosperity of the West we have been sheltered from hardship and this has led to a poor understanding of the place of suffering in the life of believers. God's word clearly shows us that suffering is a normal part of the Christian life.[11]

We need a genuine Christian answer to some of these questions rather than offering a weak or superficial reply to someone who is suffering. Being brave can mean asking these large questions that may overshadow the horizon for a while. *We need a platform to allow people to ask those large questions:*

> Lord, why do I have to go through this?
> Why am I not healed when they are?
> Lord, help me understand why?

Often the reply back is: One day you will understand and on that day it will not matter.

Remember that tears are not a bad thing

If anyone has experienced a health crisis then I believe you have had to be courageous or brave for a season. I am not saying that every day you are resolute and strong, because there are times when our emotions are volatile and fragile. We should give ourselves permission to be vulnerable and allow tears to fall. Tears do not signify a lack of bravery – simply consider Jesus in the Garden of Gethsemane! Tears are very much part of our emotional response. We know that in general women cry five times more often than men although in our household the opposite is true!

It's a little-known fact that your fearfully and wonderfully made body, this incredible feat of God-created engineering that is you, produces three types of tears: basal, reflex, and emotional tears. Basal tears are produced to keep your cornea lubricated so your eyes don't dry out. Reflex tears help you to wash out any irritations to your eyes. And finally, there are the emotional, or "crying" tears that are produced in response to stress, anger, pain, etc. Amazingly, scientists have discovered that this third category of emotional tears contains a natural painkiller, called leucine enkephalin.[12] This all serves to remind us that "a good cry is good for us".

Lisa Copen concludes her *Huffpost* blog with this suggestion: "… let us not forget that we are human beings who were designed to feel fear, need affirmation and loving support, and shed tears. For myself, this is intertwined with my faith in God and knowing when to surrender *to* the emotions and when to surrender them *over*."[13]

Postscript: I got the all-clear today. I am off to Uganda on Friday. So pleased, and I will be careful.

Prayer

> Father God,
>
> I stand in awe and wonder at what Your Son went through for me.
>
> His humanity means You understand the trials I face.
>
> Thank You that You did not divorce Yourself from the struggles of life.
>
> Help me to put You first each day.
>
> Grant me courage to keep going.
>
> In Your Son's name.
>
> Amen.

CHAPTER 4

THE CHALLENGES OF PARENTHOOD

There is so much that could be said on the subject of parenthood and there is already a vast range of books, training videos, and courses on the topic, many of which are to be recommended as invaluable resources for parents. I am writing this chapter not as an expert on parenting but simply as an ordinary mother sharing some of her thoughts.

I am also conscious of those parents who have never been able to conceive their own children or who have taken the courageous decision to foster or adopt. We have such folk in our own church family and I am in awe of you. You have shown immense bravery through trying to conceive, the months of waiting, treatment, or even the loss of an embryo and the hope it would have brought. There are no words, comfort, or answers I can give you although I am convinced that God knows. I do not know the answer just as I don't know why some people never fall in love and get married. I believe that God has seen your suffering. He understands your loss. I do know that like you one day – having had a miscarriage at an early stage – we will see our lost children in Heaven.

As a midwife, I was able to see the problems people faced in more vivid detail as I worked in the early pregnancy unit. I also delivered babies who were able to capture life's breath only for a minute. I do know that God was there in those moments, giving strength and showing empathy for human suffering. This is not a textbook or a course: it is simply a reminder that we all go through times or seasons in our lives that are difficult. And sometimes the scars can remain with us for life.

Children with additional needs

None of us knows where the journey will take us when we discover we are having a child. It is a journey of trusting daily that our baby will develop and grow as they should. Sometimes that journey takes a dramatic twist. I remember once, as a midwife, working on night duty being with a young couple while the woman was in labour. I realized quite quickly into the delivery that there was a problem as the baby was either in an awkward presentation or there was something seriously wrong. I managed to call someone to contact the paediatrician – actually insisting that they wake the consultant and ask him to come in. While I was waiting for the team to arrive I delivered the baby and it was obvious that this beautiful baby boy had some terrible disabilities. To the parents he was their long hoped-for child. The emotion in the room changed from excitement and anticipation to anxiety and loss with the realization that he was not a healthy baby. To the couple he was still their baby boy no matter what was wrong, but they were frightened at the possible implications of his disabilities. They were so brave. We shared a few precious moments before the medical team arrived: grief and celebration became interwoven and tears of joy and sadness were shed.

I had told them earlier in the evening that Malcolm, my husband, was a minister so they asked me to pray with them. It was a special time. About a year later Malcolm was visiting a member of our congregation in the intensive care ward. A young lady sitting beside the bed next to the patient Malcolm was visiting asked him to pray for her husband as he had been in an accident and was acutely ill. She went on to explain that she knew who he was as I had cared for them both when their son was born. Their baby boy lived for only twenty-four hours but they had time to hold him, get the family in to meet him, and choose his name. She remembers me telling her that to God he was perfect and as valuable to Him as they were.

Sometimes a child is born but with additional needs that implode in the centre of our families and neatly timetabled world.

Becoming parents

Our personal journey into parenthood started quite early on in our married life. We knew that Malcolm was called to Bible college and we had a choice: to plan for children before or after college. We both trusted God for the earlier rather than the later option. I was twenty-five and Malcolm twenty-three when our first son Matthew arrived in July 1993. As a midwife I had knowledge of pregnancy and childbirth but not of parenthood. The day after Matthew was born and everyone had gone home I looked at this beautiful tiny baby in the cot and I stood and cried, knowing this was God's child and we were to be caretakers for Him. The load of responsibility weighed heavily on my shoulders.

Then in 1995 Benjamin was born with the loudest cry of any of our children before or since. His two sisters followed few years later. Benjamin's life has been overshadowed by ill health and in his early years he had so many visits to hospital we were given open or direct access to the children's ward. His bubbly character, resilience, and tenacity have meant that he has kept fighting even when Malcolm and I were weary. I do not know the cost of parenting a child with disabilities but having cared for a child with additional needs I am conscious that the cost must be high. We struggled juggling family, church, work, and the visits back and forth to hospital. We were stretched in every way when Benjamin had another bout of pneumonia. Our biggest challenge was keeping the family together.

There are some dates that stick in the mind: 22 November 1963 when J. F. Kennedy was assassinated, November 1989 when the Berlin Wall came down, and 11 September 2001 when the Twin Towers were destroyed. Our oldest son remembers being in the hospital with Benjamin when I called to tell them that one of the Twin Towers had been struck. Matthew was only seven years old.

What the Bible says about unexpected challenges

Benjamin faced challenges that we did not expect him to have. Through the years I cried to God. On a number of occasions I thought we would lose him. During one particularly difficult time our church family met and prayed for him. One of the elders rang after the prayer meeting while we were at the hospital to tell us he had a word for us. Although he quoted the words from Deuteronomy 33:12 to my husband he clearly told him that it was taken from Deuteronomy 31:11. Malcolm got him to read 33:12 to him. The NIV says,

About Benjamin he said:

"Let the beloved of the Lord rest secure in him,
for he shields him all day long,
and the one the Lord loves rests between his
shoulders."

We were amazed. We could not stop crying – not because Benjamin had suddenly improved but because we had been reminded that God was there in the midst of all that was going on. We also had to let God gently carry our son because first and foremost Benjamin was God's son.

God doesn't tell us we will have a better life if we trust Him: He simply reminds us that life will be better with Him at the centre. We can trust Him and rest in the shadow of His wings even when we are at the end of ourselves, which is the place where there is always more of Him. And He absolutely knows what it is like to see a child suffer or to lose a son in the worst way possible.

In Jesus' manifesto in the Sermon on the Mount (Matthew chapter 5) He said:

> *"You're blessed when you're at the end of your rope. With less of you there is more of God and his rule.*
>
> *"You're blessed when you feel you've lost what is most dear to you. Only then can you be embraced by the One most dear to you.*
>
> *"You're blessed when you're content with just who you are – no more, no less. That's the moment you find yourselves proud owners of everything that can't be bought.*
>
> *"You're blessed when you've worked up a good appetite for God. He's food and drink in the best meal you'll ever eat.*
>
> *"You're blessed when you care. At the moment of being 'care-full,' you find yourselves cared for.*
>
> *"You're blessed when you get your inside world – your mind and heart – put right. Then you can see God in the outside world.*
>
> *"You're blessed when you can show people how to cooperate instead of compete or fight. That's when you discover who you really are, and your place in God's family.*
>
> *"You're blessed when your commitment to God*

*provokes persecution. The persecution drives you
even deeper into God's kingdom.*

*"Not only that – count yourselves blessed every time
people put you down or throw you out or speak
lies about you to discredit me. What it means is
that the truth is too close for comfort and they are
uncomfortable. You can be glad when that happens
– give a cheer, even! – for though they don't like it, I
do! And all heaven applauds. And know that you are
in good company. My prophets and witnesses have
always gotten into this kind of trouble."*

Surviving the journey

We need God to travel with us on this journey. Living with
a child with additional needs can generate huge stresses in
the family, as reflected in the findings of various research
studies. Wymbs and Pelham suggest that the divorce rates and
predictors of divorce among parents of young people with
attention-deficit/hyperactivity disorder (ADHD) are twice as
high as in the general population, with many experiencing
divorce by the time their children are eight years old.[1] Couples
with children who have Down's syndrome frequently divorce
by the time their child reaches two years of age.[2] Often the main
caregiver feels isolated and lonely and does not feel supported
by their partner. Higher rates of divorce or separation are
also reported for parents of preterm babies[3] and in families
of children with an autism spectrum disorder.[4] These higher
figures are found right across the board and relate equally to
parents of children with physical and mental disabilities.

It is so important to remember that families of children with all kinds of additional needs are desperate for our support. These families are in our local churches and communities where we should be the visible presence of the love of Jesus through the care and support we give them. I am in awe of these parents – their whole lives are impacted by the needs of their children. When I think of courage – of bravery for a season – I am reminded of a simple scene that I witnessed recently. I was going into a café with my husband and saw an older couple trying to encourage their son to go into the café despite the fact his usual table was already occupied. They were not embarrassed by the noise or disruption that was occurring. They simply spoke to their son in a calm and collected manner, trying to encourage him to take the brave step of sitting at a different seat by the window. It gave me a glimpse, an insight, into their daily lives.

The American author Debra Ginsberg has this to say about parenting:

> Through the blur, I wondered if I was alone or if other parents felt the same way I did – that everything involving our children was painful in some way. The emotions, whether they were joy, sorrow, love, or pride, were so deep and sharp that in the end they left you raw, exposed and yes, in pain. The human heart was not designed to beat outside the human body and yet, each child represented just that – a parent's heart bared, beating forever outside its chest.[5]

What can we do in terms of support?

1. Put Jesus at the centre of your family life. Set time to pray together as a family for each other. What you are experiencing affects the whole family unit.

2. Set up or be involved in a prayer/support network for parents of children with additional needs. I attended one when we lived in Reading. It was wonderful to be able to talk about some of the challenges in an open manner. I was also able to talk about some of the practical aspects such as monetary support from the government.

3. As parents of a child with additional needs, work as a team. There isn't a one-size-fits-all approach to determining roles within a family when it comes caring for your child. The key is clear and transparent communication about what is happening.

4. Do not treat your child with additional needs any differently from your other children.

5. The stress of caring for an ill child or one with additional needs can bring to the forefront stresses previously existing within a marriage but your child's illness is certainly not to blame for the problems you have.

6. Care for yourselves too. This is particularly important for the parents. Do you have a regular date night? Ensure that the date is not spoilt by talk about medical updates or work! Invest in your relationship and have fun.

7. As a church family do not see people with labels – see them as Jesus does.

8. Simply offer help to parents of children with additional needs. They don't need people to tell them what they are doing right or wrong or how to parent. Be there for them and let them know you are there to help.

I love the way Eugene Peterson paraphrases Matthew 5:7 in *The Message*: "You're blessed when you care. At the moment of being 'care-full,' you find yourselves cared for."

We have been so fortunate to be part of a church family that has shown immense care to us. As parents to four wonderful children, our life was a little hectic. We were once asked how we coped with four children under five years old. Malcolm answered: "We were just tired all the time." We have also been aware that we need to care for ourselves. We decided early on in our marriage that once a year we would have a short break to spend time together and pray, to invest in our marriage no matter what else was happening. Sometimes the practical logistics of rehoming four children for a few days was a huge challenge.

One year I won an all-expenses-paid trip to New York by writing the slogan for Foster's beer! We could manage to find friends who would care for the children but were concerned about Benjamin. He had suffered a recent bout of pneumonia and had not completed his course of intravenous antibiotics. However, his hospital consultant told us to go and the hospital staff cared for Benjamin in an amazing way. He was happy as he had a passion for their mashed potato and according to our son, "They make the most amazing mash." (He still does have a mashed potato passion and wants to have a mash bar at his wedding in December.) I remember coming back from this trip to hear people comment about the fact I went off on a holiday and left my son in hospital. We have to be so careful not to judge others. What my critics did not know was that Benjamin's medication was needed every four hours and each administration would take us a good half hour, even through the night. We were running on empty – utterly exhausted and hardly managing to care for our children let alone ourselves.

I recently had my mum down to stay. We were talking about parenthood. She confessed to not fully understanding the challenges involved in living with Benjamin until we had a family holiday in the Lake District. On the first day Benjamin became ill so we spent all day at a local hospital and had to start intravenous and nebulized medication. Mum had not realized how much we had to do until she saw it first-hand.

While she was with me I asked Mum what had been her biggest challenge as a parent. In the early days she had to struggle with the unexpected news of a twin pregnancy (only discovering she was carrying twins when she was well into her third trimester), preterm babies, and hospitalization, as well as adapting to the massive changes in her life. Dad and Mum had to navigate the wisdom of neighbours, family, friends, and even people they did not know to work out and decide how best they would parent. Mum also recalled another time that resonates with most parents: sending children off to school for the first time. Poor Mum had to watch me and my twin brother head through those school gates. Another picture was when she had to leave me in my flat at university when I was just seventeen. Coming down the stairs, she passed people with mad haircuts and crazy clothes and wondered how a child brought up in rural Scotland would cope with big city life!

Dealing with an empty nest

I also asked people on my author's Facebook page what they felt their biggest challenge was. When did they need the most courage? The overwhelming response was: letting children go. When our oldest son went to university Malcolm and I were a mess! We were asked how we would ever cope with the transition to the empty-nest syndrome. We still have one daughter at home but we are currently preparing for the complete version of empty-nest syndrome! This well-known phenomenon describes the feelings of grief and sometimes loneliness parents feel when their children leave home. I think all parents are susceptible to this. Some factors make it worse, such as basing your primary identity on being a parent. Symptoms can include depression, a sense of loss of purpose, stress, anxiety, and rejection.

My mum says that she felt that the hardest part in all this was the relinquishing of control. To be honest, this is something both parents and children struggle with as they go through major periods of transition. We need open and transparent communication to transition well.

I also sense that we are in a changing culture with a boomerang generation as children often return home after attending university because they cannot afford to get on the housing ladder straight away. In 2015 around 40 per cent of young adults aged fifteen to thirty-four in the UK were living with their parents.[6] Only a decade earlier, just 15 per cent of men and 8 per cent of women in that age range lived at home. Our oldest son is now home finishing his master's dissertation and we have had long chats about what it would look like living at home again. (Of course, we have had a few trial runs as our children have returned home from study for their long summer breaks.)

For the majority of families, the departure of the last child from the household has been shown to lead to positive changes in parental mood state related to a reduction in the daily hassles of life.[7] Essentially, the conclusion is that life becomes quieter and this is a good thing! If, however, the transition to the empty nest is not managed well, this can cause raised levels of anxiety and depression for up to two years after the child has left.[8]

Here are a few suggestions on how we can prepare ourselves and our children for this major change in all our lives:

- Facilitate the transition. Simple things like ensuring they can cook, perhaps by having cooking lessons through the summer months prior to going to university. We ensured that our children were cooking the family meals regularly and were also involved in shopping and budgeting for them. I often met students at work who admitted to not being able to cook for themselves. Jess Denham's report for *The Independent* suggests that one in ten students never cook for themselves during term time. A quarter will splash out on a takeaway every single week.[9] Bryony Gordon and Simon Hogg in *The Daily Telegraph* report that today's university students could be the unhealthiest yet as many undergraduates are eating poorly due to a lack of basic cookery skills.[10]

- Don't leave everything until the last minute – start collecting what they need several months in advance.

- Be honest about how you are feeling. Acknowledge your grief.

- Talk with your partner.

- Seek advice and support from friends and family who understand how you feel.

- Give yourself time to adapt to the changes.

- Plan some exciting events for the weeks after your child leaves. Perhaps a few days away or a much-needed holiday?

- Take an interest in hobbies and activities you have more time for. I have a long list of things I want to do. Some of them are things I want to do with my husband.

- Keep a journal.

- Don't make any big decisions. We once bought a sofa and after a year we regretted the decision. We realized we had bought it during a time of turmoil. We had not been thinking straight.

- Look after yourself! That includes healthy eating, and exercising and your regular quiet time.

- Remember we are all different and react in different ways.

- Seek help if you feel overwhelmed.

There are many memorable events we go through as parents. My boys have never forgotten the time I was so angry that I threw their hand-held games console down the stairs because they would not tidy up their rooms. I am ashamed that I allowed my frustration to vent itself in this way. They also, however, remember the times when we made a den and a campfire in the garden and cooked sausages, and when Malcolm and I surprised them with a trip to Euro Disney after living in a trailer tent for over a month.

I know beyond a shadow of doubt that I have been anything but a perfect parent. As a couple, we repeatedly said: "We've never done this before." However, I do know that it has been the area of my life where I have had to draw on the deepest reserves of the courage that God gives. Time and again, I have had to go and lay all at my Saviour's feet, as I pray for the family. He hears, He listens, and He is there.

Prayer

Thank you, Father, that You are ever-present.

You know when we rise and when we sit down. You know when life is so busy that we struggle to make time to listen. You know when our lives are not as we expected them to be.

Help us to keep in rhythm with You and what You want us to do. Help us trust You for our families.

In Jesus' name.

Amen.

CHAPTER 5

FACING RETIREMENT

One of the first times I was asked to preach and teach on this topic was to a ladies' meeting at another church. When I got there I discovered that there were probably about eighty plus ladies present who all looked at least twice my age. My topic was "What's Heaven?" I came away laughing to myself thinking that in the ordinary scheme of things you just would not choose that topic for your seniors' group. God graciously was able to use it.

So when it came to the chapter of this book I knew I wanted to highlight the need for bravery when facing retirement, but I knew I was not the person to do it. I had to ask someone to write it for me. Barbara reminds me of the woman in the poem, "Warning" by Jenny Joseph. She is funny, has immense resilience, and has the spirit captured in the poem. She is also on this journey. Barbara is a dear friend, prayer warrior, and a member of our church family. Her words ring true with experience and faith. I hope you enjoy reading this chapter as much as I did.

When I am an old woman I shall wear purple
With a red hat that doesn't go, and doesn't suit me.
And I shall spend my pension
on brandy and summer gloves
And satin sandals,
and say we've no money for butter.
I shall sit down on the pavement when I am tired,
And gobble up samples in shops and press alarm
bells,
And run my stick along the public railings,
And make up for the sobriety of my youth.
I shall go out in my slippers in the rain
And pick the flowers in other people's gardens,
And learn to spit.

You can wear terrible shirts and grow more fat,
And eat three pounds of sausages at a go,
Or only bread and pickle for a week,
And hoard pens and pencils and beer mats
and things in boxes.

But now we must have clothes that keep us dry,
And pay our rent and not swear in the street,
And set a good example for the children.
We will have friends to dinner and read the papers.

But maybe I ought to practise a little now?
So people who know me
are not too shocked and surprised,
When suddenly I am old
and start to wear purple!

Jenny Joseph (b. 1932)

Enjoy! Debbie

Focusing on God's will for the next stage of our life

Barbara Graham

James Packer writes in his book, *Finishing Our Course with Joy*, of the three stages of aging: "young olds" (65–75); "medium olds" (75–85); and "oldest olds" (85+).[1] Our present-day retirement age of leaving work and paid employment means we usually fall into the "young old" classification. I am seventy-two and a "young old". As we enter the new world of retirement, we begin another journey. This journey may well be the best of our lives or not, but we travel with many others. We are not alone.

Three years ago Eric, my husband, and I spoke with two older ladies about the coming changes in their lives. Judy, one of the ladies, said to us, "Remember it is 're-tyre-ment' not 'retirement'." I was amused but also challenged to prepare properly for the road ahead.

Judy died last year at 101. She and her friend Fran started a wonderful retreat centre when Judy was seventy-five! "The House of Bread" is a place of peace in the Cotswolds near Shakespeare's Stratford-upon-Avon. It is a place of quietness, filled with the gentle loveliness of Christ where people become reconnected with God.

Judy urged us never to stop reaching out for God's will as we make our plans for the next stage of life and to seek always what He has in mind for our lives, whatever our age and circumstances. We are each so different with our gifts and abilities, our health and resources, our family circumstances, our past, and our present. God has uniquely made us to desire and find His will at every stage of our lives, not least in our retirement and as we progress into the later years. God plants within each of our hearts the desire to live a life of value. For the Christian believer, it is the desire to live a life that glorifies Him whatever our age.

Opportunities in later life

Unless you are unwell, being a "young old" can give you space to think through the past. What things went well and were productive and what things were simply a waste of your time and effort? Reassessing your priorities and deciding on a viable future lifestyle is essential. What opportunities do you have now you are no longer in the fast lane? Usually the need to provide for a growing family is no longer our priority as we age. Eric keeps reminding me that we never have to be in a hurry ever again! Time is a wonderful gift from God and retirement is the golden opportunity to use it more wisely. Thinking through things can lead to a late flowering, a determined desire to do better, serve better, love more, care more, and not to get caught up in unnecessary, mindless activities.

After a lifetime of activity in the UK and abroad, a time of reflection has been a welcome oasis to us. Yet one rarely stays at an oasis, it is just a place of refreshment before continuing the journey. This time can be a window in our lives to think through what really matters to us and make any needed changes before the onward journey into the future.

There are many ways to use the time of freedom from constant activity of our middle years. I believe Eric's father Jon is an example of a person who used his time wisely.

Jon was a hardworking dairy farmer in County Fermanagh, Northern Ireland. Life was an endless round of getting up early and going to bed late. The animals needed to come first. It was a heavy commitment day in and day out. The family all went to church as they could, but time was always at a premium. Around his sixty-fifth birthday, Jon handed over the running of the farm to his eldest son and bravely began a new pace of life after a lifetime of busyness. The most noticeable thing he did was to begin to regularly read his Bible and the Book of Common Prayer. He was determined that his last days should be given to seeking and finding God in a new way. And he did! One day he was tuning his radio and for the first time he heard a Christian radio station. After that he and Eric's mother listened regularly and grew in faith. They began to read Christian books and share the things they learned with the people who came to the house – even Jon's carers as he aged. Life for Jon took on a fresh dimension in his later years.

Retirement and the present culture

There are many aspects of retirement that are actually conditioned by our prevalent culture. The media, modern books, and films all seem to encourage us to overindulge ourselves when we retire. We now have freedom to do whatever gives us pleasure. To quote Packer again: "Retirees are admonished, both explicitly and implicitly, in terms that boil down to: Relax. Slow down. Take it easy. Amuse yourself. Do only what you enjoy… You are off the treadmill and out of the rat race. Now at last you are your own man or woman and can concentrate on having fun… Enjoy yourself."

As I write these words I am not surprised that some eventually find retirement after work boring and feel useless, then move into depression and even lose interest in life. It is a trap we can all fall into but it is a trap to be avoided. C. S. Lewis wrote in his adult fantasy *Perelandra*: "To walk out of His will is to walk into nowhere." Concentrating solely on ourselves means we end up meandering into nowhere of true value. I don't mean we should never have a holiday or other pleasurable activities, indeed Jesus and His disciples took time out to recoup and be restored and refreshed. It is just that self-indulgence can be self-destroying. It takes a brave and determined person to walk away from ourselves and our own concerns to seek a better focus for the future.

Our future contentment simply lies where our focus is. We can now focus even more on our relationship with God, those we love, and those who need love. It takes courage to do something different. It may well be sitting quietly, meditating or praying. It could be starting or assisting in a club for the "oldest olds". It could be having a coffee morning to discuss issues we have never had time for before and help assuage the loneliness of other people as well as our own. It could be reading a favourite book to a cuddling grandchild. Pleasing God and others becomes a wonderful opportunity to relax into the presence and joy of God. We may need to bravely step out of our comfort zone but the ensuing contentment feeds our strength and fills us with hope. The courage to be different from what we were before brings freshness into our lives.

A phrase I came across recently was "Inner enoughness" – the state of being totally content with God and all He has given and will give. Is an ongoing relationship with the living, creative God, through faith in Christ, worthwhile? Can this glorious God be enough for us after forty plus years of endless activity? Of course He can!

Sometimes we really have no idea what to do or there is too much choice or too little. Be brave and ask for help and advice. Sometimes there is underlying pride because of past achievement and going to someone can make us feel inadequate. Ignore negative thoughts and ask! You will find that you are starting out afresh, and as C. S. Lewis says you will be "surprised by joy".

Retired but fit

As we enter this new and sometimes frightening stage of life, we can become confused or even paralysed with apprehension. If we have not made provision for the possibly many years ahead, then financial restraints cause concern and worry sets in. As we live so much longer than our ancestors, we can regret being forced to leave work while still fit and may feel deeply the loss of status given through our roles in society. Sometimes we lose not only the daily routine but may need to make further dramatic changes. Just as we need to prepare for death, we need to face practical problems like loss of income and downsizing. This can involve moving into new neighbourhoods, changing churches if a believer, or even a new country. Facing our future with courage does mean preparation and acceptance of a new way of life.

To become a couch potato is not the best option for the fit and vital retiree. In fact, it can lead to becoming unwell and depressed. There are many possibilities for the fit retiree. Doing something new, something dreamed of in the past, may take a special kind of courage. To step out of your comfort zone to join a night class or a day class to learn that new language, to study astronomy or theology – all take courage but may give you an interest which expands your thinking and fulfilment.

Using your latent gifts to fulfil your desire to produce something beautiful can be so satisfying. Take a pottery or drawing class or a creative writing course and finally produce that book of poems you always wanted to do. To go on a photography course, or do an Open University degree in archaeology or engineering, or simply learning more about your computer can inspire and excite you as you get up each day.

Volunteering in the charity sector or at church provides an equally satisfying "joy in the morning" feeling. Use your past skills to help or encourage others. Many a mission organization enjoys the volunteering of older people. Relating to younger people and sharing your wisdom becomes a meaningful, mentoring experience. And be assured you do have wisdom! Those grey hairs mean experience! Working through the inevitable problems of the past life and sharing outcomes can help others, especially when sharing our failures and God's forgiveness and restoration. Indeed, listening to other people can be one of the greatest blessings of having time available. Even grandchildren are glad for someone to listen. One of my personal joys after picking up my young granddaughters from school is, as we walk home hand in hand through a woodland pathway, listening to Ella and Eve vying with each other to tell me their news. They learn to listen to each other too.

Facing the future with honesty

While able to, we do need to honestly consider the future and further aging. We need to bravely face the need to prepare for our long-term care, making our wills, sorting out power of attorney, and making sure our families or friends will know what to do if there is sudden or gradual decline. These issues all need our attention as we move into the later years. Even preparing for our funeral services helps the grieving left-behinds. Putting our heads in the sand because we are in good health now does not help anyone. Moving closer to family or friends is far better done sooner rather than too late.

As we face the realities of the latter years, we need to do it with courage and honesty. Sharing with others who are facing the same concerns can be so helpful. Praying together over our particular circumstances can lead to closer relationships and provide much-needed friendships as family and friends die and loneliness peeps in the window. Bravely caring for one another, despite our own problems, now takes on an even greater importance.

But when there is deterioration in health or faculties, if dementia or serious illness takes away the former security, then there does need to be a much deeper acceptance of the new way of life. From the experience of dementia in my own family, I know that dementia does not take away faith even if it can no longer be expressed. Our spirits are forever entwined with God's Spirit if we trust in Jesus. Reminding each other of the glowing future ahead is something we can each do for another, even if there seems to be no response. John, in Revelation 21:3–4 declared, "and God himself will be with them and be their God. He will wipe away every tear from their eyes. There will be no more death, or mourning or crying or pain, for the old order of things has passed away."

Facing the end of the race

Two very different people I know replied the same thing when I asked what I could pray for them: "Please pray I can end the race well." Jim was a much-loved pastor and outstanding preacher, well known in UK Christian circles and overseas. He lived a long, fruitful life serving God. Jim was a particularly gifted teacher of God's word at his own church fellowship, in conferences, and one to one. He lived to see thousands of people respond in growing faith and holiness. His interest in overseas mission led to a personal ministry in Korea training pastors and encouraged many training for ministry in this country and overseas.

Beryl is a long-time personal friend who has been disabled from birth. She lives her life alone quietly struggling to even climb the stairs. Walking and talking are incredibly difficult daily tasks. Her parents are now long dead, but despite being in constant pain every day, her faith shines through every encounter with her. Beryl is a Christ-centred person, almost seventy now, hidden away from most people and unknown outside a small circle of friends. Her life is filled with prayerful intercession and the reading of God's word. Despite her frailty and aging, Beryl's reply to my question was exactly the same as Jim's: "Let me finish the race well."

Jim was facing cancer and Beryl faces intense daily pain and disability but their request was to finish the race well. They could have asked prayer for many other things like healing, strength, finances, new things to "do", more visitors, and a multitude of extra blessings to give a more pleasant life, but they didn't. Both wanted to please God to the end of their unique lives. They both bravely asked for something that would give God honour and glory. And He did!

Paul writes in 1 Corinthians 9:24–26: "Do you not know that in a race all the runners run, but only one receives the prize? So run that you may obtain it. Every athlete exercises self-control in all things... So I do not run aimlessly..." (ESV).

We are each running the race of life. Most of us do not opt out of life even if ill or discouraged. Tragically, some folk do take the extreme way out, but death is never the end for them or for us. God is still there, waiting our final, amazing encounter with Him. Paul knows this and so he urges us to run to win the prize at the end of the race. Like our present-day Olympians and Paralympians, who train relentlessly to gain what they want, we too are urged to keep going.

It takes courage as well as determination to sometimes put one foot in front of the other each day when, like my friend Beryl, you live in constant pain or feel engulfed by grief or sorrow. Loneliness and all kinds of loss can distract us from the race we would really like to be running. Letting go of our past is as important as looking to the future.

As we face the finishing lap, we can take valuable time on reviewing our inner lives. It takes a brave man or woman to look inside ourselves and see who we really are. It takes courage and humility to ask God to review us and forgive us. We may well find God's standards different from ours. We daily have the opportunity to start afresh with Him. Even if we have not been inside a church for the past fifty or sixty years, we can begin again. Coming to know Jesus as Saviour and Lord gives us new life at any age. It is never too late to begin the road to hope and joy. If unsure, ask a friend to help. It takes courage from deep within to express your need of someone more than yourself. We need to care for ourselves physically, mentally, and spiritually.

The pathway ahead is clearly marked, even if it is bumpy sometimes. The Bible is sometimes called God's life manual. Reading it gives constant insight into how to live in contentment and satisfaction as we love and serve God to the end of our days. Reaching out to God in prayer day by day comforts and strengthens us. Interceding for others takes our focus off ourselves and we see many a miracle to rejoice in.

God wants to be in relationship with us so in one sense we are never ever alone. Serving Him in whatever way He indicates for us as individuals, will give increased and lasting purpose to the very end before our wonderful welcome home.

Prayer

Father,

Thank you that You are our Father. Thank you that we can trust You.

Help us to make You the focus of our lives. As we move into our future, please be close to us and lead us along Your chosen pathway for our later lives. Please give us courage to face whatever lies ahead. Please help us to make every day count for You until we see You face to face.

Amen.

CHAPTER 6

BRAVERY THROUGH THE SEASONS

By Debbie and Matthew Duncan

I suppose I never thought about the stage of my life I am now in before and that is why I want to spend some time writing about it. I married young and was pregnant with our oldest child within a year of marriage. We then had our four children quite close together. With four children I have had the pleasure and wonder to watch them grow up, trusting, and praying for their future. As a family we have prayed that they would remain close to Jesus. Each child is unique and each has a personal relationship with God, which we can be thankful for. Like any family going through this season that requires a brave heart Malcolm and I have had to trust them to God again and again.

The sandwich generation

All of a sudden, however, we have found ourselves in a season that is a little different than the one we expected. We always knew that there would be a time when we stand looking forward with hope at our children and their futures. What we did not expect was to also stand facing backwards trying to be brave for our parents as we see shadows pass over their lives.

Within the last fifteen years Malcolm has grieved the passing of both parents and I am experiencing the protracted journey of grief that early onset Alzheimer's brings.

So now I feel like I am juggling lots of balls. They whizz around my head: Can Anna pay her rent? Can I take time off to see Mum and Dad? Will Riodhna pass her driving test? Will Matthew get the job he is applying for? I hope Dad's tests are negative. I hope the wedding plans are going OK. And: How can I cope? It sometimes feels that I am being stretched in so many directions that I may just implode. In all honesty, as I say, I just did not think that I would be in this place just now. I thought that I would not have to worry about my parents until a little further down the road.

Paula Banks, in her parenting blog, calls those of us in this situation as the "sandwich generation". She goes on to suggest that, "There's almost nothing more draining, stressful, emotional and guilt-inducing than caring for an elderly parent or relative while raising kids."[1]

This term, the "sandwich generation", was first used in the 1980s by social worker Dorothy Miller to describe women in their thirties and forties who were taking care of both their children and their parents. It was also used to describe a subset of the baby boomers. The baby boomers tend to marry later in life and have children in their mid- to late thirties. They have therefore become the first generation to be "sandwiched" between the care of adult children and their parents. The numbers are rising as there are approximately 20 million women in the UK between the ages of forty-five and fifty-six, 10 per cent of which have children and are also caring for older relatives. Women are predominately the main carers but add in men who are doing the same and the numbers jump considerably.[2] According to the Pew Research Center this equates to just over one in eight Americans aged forty to sixty raising a child and caring for a parent.[3] That actually means that just under a quarter of all adults in their forties or fifties who have at least one parent age sixty-five or older are supporting their parents in some way.

Carol Abaya, journalist and writer about the sandwich generation categorized the different types of people falling into this category as:

- **Traditional:** those who are sandwiched between aging parents who need care and who are helping their own children.

- **Club Sandwich:** those individuals who are in their fifties or sixties sandwiched between aging parents, adult children, and even grandchildren. This also includes people in their thirties and forties who may have young children, aging parents, and grandparents.

- **Open Faced:** this includes anyone else involved in care of the elderly.[4]

The numbers are growing due to increased life expectancy, people having children later in life, and smaller family units with fewer siblings to share in providing care for elderly parents.

Families are also more fractured and separated by distance then they ever used to be. I think we also have to consider the financial economy. When my husband and I had our four children tuition fees for university were only about £1,000. Now our children leave university with a bill of £27,000 for tuition fees alone – that does not include their rent and living costs. The debt of a university education is strapped to their ankles as they emerge into the workplace and full independence. Many return home to be supported until they can afford to rent or buy their own homes. I am not complaining – I love the fact that our eldest son is now home as he hunts for a job – I am just reminding us of the situations many parents find themselves in.

Consider the costs

There are many costs that go along with being a sandwich generation caregiver. These vary from stress, financial burden, and even burnout. There is often a higher cost if you need to move your parents or in-laws in with you. It can be a rewarding experience or a real stress, and can be dependent on a variety of variables, including the amount of care they need, the type of care, and even personality types. It is a highly emotive topic and potentially opens up a vast cavern of guilt. A decision not to have a parent move in can feel like ingratitude and grossly selfish, especially if we have friends who have had their family live with them.

If you find yourself in this position trying to decide how best to care for elderly parents, ask for God's wisdom to help you with your decision. I cannot tell you what to do, but I do know that everyone's circumstances are different.

You may have relatives whose health is currently starting to decline. I think in these circumstances it is important to do some forward planning while your parents are relatively fit. There are obviously lots of options. It may not be feasible to have them stay long term so look at all the options from sheltered housing for the more fit and able to residential care or care in their own homes. Talk to social services. Seek advice.

Despite these consequential costs many caregivers who look after both their children and their aging parents report that 52 per cent say they are pretty happy with their lives – higher, that is, than those not in this season.[5]

I would love to have more time to be involved in my parents' lives. I am fortunate to have an amazing sister who does so much more for them than I do as she lives much closer to them than me. I am in awe of all she does. It is an act of love isn't it – caring for your parents? I am so fortunate to know that my parents love me. There are some families who have embraced their parents despite the fact that they have a fractured relationship. In fact, some would argue that the sandwich generation have an obligation to care for their aging parents. Whether it is due to a sense of obligation or of love, the Bible is clear: "Honour your father and mother, so that you may live long in the land the Lord your God is giving you" (Exodus 20:12). This is the only one of the Ten Commandments that is attached to a promise.

You are a caregiver for a season. No one can tell you how long you will be in this place. I can tell you that Jesus will be with you. You will find it difficult at times; there will be challenges. Share the load with your partner. Talk, talk, talk – about what it involves and how you can support each other.

Make a plan and revisit it on a monthly basis as to how you are going to visit parents and support your children at the same time.

Try to make your life easy. That includes technology. We use technology to stay in touch with our family and friends. Sometimes you are so busy sorting out a situation you find yourself in that you discover you have not told everyone about it. Days later people say to you, "You should have told me, I could have helped." You can be so busy putting out fires you don't have time to plan or even think about the future. To help us navigate these times we started a WhatsApp group for close family members. We still use it – sometimes on a daily basis. Any last-minute prayers, worries, or concerns gets shared on it. I know that my family will pray if I add anything on it.

You also need to care for your own needs. You are a person who consists of body, heart, and soul. All those areas need to be looked after. In caring for your physical side, I am talking about sleeping, eating, resting and exercising; for your spiritual side: praying, reading, or listening to Scripture, and fellowship; for your mental side: share your anxieties and concerns. Identify stressors and try to reduce them. There is so much more I can say but I think you get the picture.

Life will be difficult. Remember what Jesus said in the Sermon on the Mount in Matthew 6:3, 7: "You're blessed when you're at the end of your rope. With less of you there is more of God and his rule" and, "You're blessed when you care. At the moment of being 'care-full', you find yourselves cared for."

How can we be brave and keep all the balls in the air? I have listed a few suggestions below:

1. **Stop and take a deep breath.** You do need to make sure you have time to stop and breathe. The Hebrew name for God is Yahweh. It is comprised of aspirated consonants. When spoken aloud they are similar to the sound you make when you breathe. Every time you take a breath in and out you are saying His name.

2. **Look after yourself** – physically, spiritually, mentally.

3. **Do not hold on to guilt.** You will fail to keep those balls in the air. You are not perfect and cannot do this by yourself. If you do not manage everything you want to do, then don't worry.

4. **Get the whole family involved.** Let everyone know what is happening. There will be days when you are so busy you cannot phone your parents for your daily chat – ask your children to phone. You are not indispensable.

5. **It is not wrong to ask for help.** Generally people love to be asked. You may need to ask your church family, the charitable sector, or social services to help. Get all the support you can.

6. **Be grateful for what you achieve.** Be thankful even for little achievements. Some days I am just glad that I can get dressed and keep the house running as it should. My ironing basket overflows or the garden is a mess but they are not my priorities.

7. **Do not feel guilty in saying no.** I have had to step down from a variety of volunteer roles in church. This is the season that I am in. I don't know if I will be able to go back to what I was doing before. For now I am content in what God wants me to do.

Whether you are an open sandwich or a classic traditional one, it does help to understand how all those individuals involved in your situation feel. Listen to what they have to say and how they feel about the changes in their circumstances. The first half of this chapter has been about how I feel and the lessons I have learned. Matthew, our oldest son, is now going to open the door to "where he is at".

Looking forward

Matthew Duncan

I'm only twenty-three but going to university remains the time in my life that required the most bravery and courage. I only made the concrete decision about a week before the university term was due to start; in fact I intended to take a gap year and even had a job lined up for that time. I was in the car with my parents going for food in late September 2012 when we heard a news bulletin on the radio about lower entry numbers for universities that year – mine was the first year that the £9,000 fees had been introduced.

While I understand university is not for everyone I was at a place in life where I was somewhat lost. I didn't know what I wanted to do going forward and I'd spent the previous two years in a sixth form that I didn't enjoy, doing A levels built around a specific path to try and get into medicine. About a year or so after starting my A levels I realized that I was heading down the wrong path. I couldn't get to grips with the subjects I was studying and no longer wanted to head down the medicine route, yet I had boxed myself into a corner, which was only worsened by the results I ended up getting at the end of my first year. So, I found a part-time job that wasn't related to what I wanted to do and came to grips with the fact that I was just going to be plodding along, no clear direction or end goal in sight. No one would take me with my results and even if they did I didn't want to spend another portion of my life dedicated to a field and area that I had no passion for.

When we heard the bulletin in the car my parents told me that I should try to apply for university courses in history – something I had always been told I was good at. In fact, the exchange ended up being quite heated and I resisted. I thought that no one would want to take me and I didn't think that I would be good enough to go anywhere anyway. When we eventually made it home they were still on my case so, in an effort to appease them, I rang up Keele University to enquire about their humanities foundation year, an area of study that my parents had told me I should have done at A level anyway, but I had disregarded them at the time.

I thought I wouldn't get the place but if it would get my parents off my back then it was worth the call. I was given a phone interview and told that this year was full but that they would possibly consider me for the next year depending on the calibre of other students that applied. Less than an hour later I received a call back. They offered me a place starting the next week on a four-year history and philosophy course, on the condition that I did the foundation year. I was to start in six days' time and the university was 150 miles away from where we lived.

I remember clearly my sister going out to the shop before I called Keele. I was going to be living at home. I had told everyone that I was staying put; nothing in my life had pointed to anything otherwise. When she returned an hour later my mum was already looking for cutlery that I could take from our house for the next four years, and my dad was trying to sort out somewhere for me to live. Things moved fast.

Praying for courage

I didn't have time to let the prospect of university sink in as I'd assumed for the better part of a year at this point that it would never happen. Even in the days leading up to the move my parents and I were frantically organizing accommodation and even stationery. I didn't initially even know where Keele was; I'd never seen nor heard of the place and I certainly didn't know anyone going there. The week sped past and on the Saturday morning my parents dropped me off at my shared accommodation. We moved the boxes in, prayed, and then they left. I was alone in my new room in my new world. I didn't know anyone and my entire life for at least the next year was packed inside a mixture of bags for life and old plastic boxes.

The next few weeks for me were some of the scariest of my life. Up until then I had never been someone who made friends particularly easily. I knew everyone else heading to university for the first time was in the same boat but it wasn't until I was actually at sea that the reality kicked in for me. Here I was, a sometimes socially awkward teen legally classified as an adult and I was scared about meeting people. I didn't know what I was doing or even how to go about it. So, I bit the bullet and prayed for courage and bravery and just started knocking on people's doors in my accommodation block – something that I would never have even considered at that time in my life.

As I write this now, almost five years to the day I left home, I have a degree in history and philosophy from Keele University, a pending Masters in journalism, media and communication, and friends that will last a lifetime. Over the last five years I've had the worst and the best experiences of my life, but most importantly I have a faith that is wildly different to when I first started out.

I know university isn't the be-all and end-all but for me the experience of having to trust in both God and other people was something that has fundamentally changed who I am as a person. They say that God has a sense of humour and in my case this is certainly true. I was always against any form of change, something that has loosened over the previous half decade. I was the family member who never wanted to move house because I worried that I'd never make new friends, let alone move over a hundred miles away to place that until this point was best known for its service station on the M6. I couldn't have done it without my family and friends but most significantly, God. If it wasn't for Him I would never have been brave enough. Within a week I had experienced situations that I never even realized existed and the change was almost instant.

I am not a self-congratulatory person in any way, but it was the point in my life that required more bravery than ever before. I wasn't saving a life or being heroic but I was challenged to shake off a core aspect of my personality that had restricted me all my life. Whenever we had moved house it was because my family wanted to; whenever I started a new school and had to make friends I waited for other people to approach me. I have not had a sheltered upbringing and I have done many things in my life that I could look back on and say required bravery but they had all been in different forms. The bravery I needed here changed me as a person – God changed me as a person. I was moving away from my family and friends and it was God who allowed me to take the leap of faith in every step of the journey.

Like many my age, both then and now, I was in a place where I didn't know what to do and was under immense pressure to have the next few decades of my life plotted out. I was just entering adulthood yet was expected to know what I would be doing within five years. As kids you are spoon-fed in school and always have something for the near future whether that is moving into secondary school or even going on to study A levels. In many ways I am still in that situation: I have recently finished my Masters in Cardiff and I'm on the hunt for jobs. I am one of the boomerang generation who is at home again with his parents. I don't know where I will be in six months' time and I'm even less certain when that changes to years. One thing I am certain of, however, is that God has a plan for me and despite the apprehensions I hold I can always look back to that September of 2012 when a young man who felt lost in the world trusted God despite everything and took a leap of faith.

Bravery is a fundamental aspect of life at any age but as both a child and young man looking to make his mark on the world it is more important now than it has ever been. I am not a brave man on my own but with God's help I am moving in the right direction. It's an interesting time to be home but I am glad I am here. My parents have certainly told me that it's been helpful to have me around as they navigate caring for grandparents and other family members.

* * *

I have no doubt that it has not always been easy for Matthew as he has adjusted to coming back home. Our society expects us to be independent. Certainly it's not easy either to become elderly or a parent to your parent. As Matthew has so clearly illustrated this is a season and we are all in this together. We need to trust God for what the future brings whether it is a new job, change in personal circumstance, or being stretched as we care for different generations of our families.

Prayer

Dear Lord,

Thank you that You are with us no matter what season we are in. In Your humanity You understand how we feel.

We ask for strength for each day. Help us to trust You more. Help us to know that when we are care-full we can be cared for.

In Jesus' name.

Amen.

CHAPTER 7

BRAVERY IN THE FACE OF UNCERTAINTY

We appear to be living in uncertain times; in the face of this uncertainty bravery is required. However, once you start to think about it, you quickly realize that every generation goes through periods of flux and change. Think of the Great Depression of the 1930s, World War II and the worst refugee crisis ever, or the fragile times of the 1960s when the Cuban Missile Crisis was so, so close to triggering World War III. My mind also goes back to momentous events that have surprised many people in the UK and further afield in the past twelve months. Even the professional pollsters failed to predict ahead of 23 June 2016 that 51.9 per cent of the UK electorate would vote in favour of leaving the European Union, and the emergence of Theresa May as prime minister blindsided most expert commentators on the UK political scene. There was a similar element of surprise about Donald Trump's narrow victory in the US presidential election in November 2016.

My husband and I recently watched *The Man in the High*

Castle, a gripping drama created by Frank Spotnitz and based on Philip K. Dick's 1962 novel of the same name. It gives us a glimpse into an alternative history of America predicated on what might have happened if the Nazis had won the war. In the series, which is set in the early 1960s, America is divided into the United States of the Greater Nazi Reich and the Japanese Pacific States. *The Man in the High Castle* became the most watched original series on Amazon in 2015. While we were engrossed in the programme, we chatted about how we would have felt living through World War II. Did everyday people ever wonder what it would be like in one or two years' time? And there are so many stories of brave people who fought for the freedom of home and nation.

I live quite close to Bletchley Park, World War II home to Alan Turing, the code breakers, and Colossus, the world's first programmable computer (invented by Tommy Flowers) that eventually sped up the work of deciphering the messages generated by the Enigma machines operated by the German armed forces. This code-breaking work remained hidden for decades because the individuals involved had all signed the Official Secrets Act, forbidding them to divulge any details about what they had done. There are stories of husbands and wives living in ignorance of the work their spouse did until the 1980s or even later. The work at Bletchley Park has now been celebrated in countless books, TV programmes, and films. President Eisenhower is believed to have said that the work at Bletchley Park shortened the war by two years. Perhaps we would all be speaking German were it not for the work done at Bletchley Park to decrypt the messages so powerfully encrypted by the Enigma and Tunny machines.

However, the question I *really* want to ask is how can we be brave when we are facing uncertainty?

Trusting God when we don't know the outcome

I recently spent a lovely evening chatting to Richard and Edwina, a couple from our church family. I had asked to see them after hearing the amazing life story of Nellie (Richard's grandmother, Helen Clarke), who had shown extraordinary bravery in uncertain times. Although Richard never met his grandmother, her story really impacted him as a child.

Nellie was like many other women of her generation. A seamstress who specialized in making fancy waistcoats for those of the upper classes who could afford them, she lived her life honouring her parents and attending church. On 22 March 1913 at the age of twenty-six, she married Sydney Clarke in Kentish Town Parish Church in the Diocese of North London. Little did they know that within a year World War I would be upon them and would influence their lives forever. At the beginning of 1914 the British army had approximately 710,000 men in its ranks, including army reserves. The regular army was thought to have consisted of just 80,000 men. That is fewer than the numbers killed between July and November 1917 in the bloodiest battle of the war at Passchendaele in Belgium. It is difficult to assess the exact numbers of allied troops who died during the Passchendaele campaign but is thought to be roughly 325,000 men.

Of the 5 million men who eventually joined the army, 2.67 million joined up as volunteers. That is about half of the population of modern-day Wales. Sydney Clarke was one of those men, joining the 19th Battalion, London (St Pancras). It was an unusual volunteer unit or territorial branch of the British Army and existed until 1961 when it eventually became absorbed into the Middlesex Regiment. In 1915 the battalion became a part of the 141st Brigade in the 47th (2nd London) Division. By the time Sydney enlisted in 1916 the regiment had been very successful in attracting the working-class men of Camden, Kentish Town, and the Euston Road area of London who wanted to fight for king and country.

Sydney Clarke's main role during the war was to lob grenades at the enemy. Being a keen sportsman, his superiors discovered that he was good at cricket and had an excellent throw. His father had been an accomplished sportsman and, according to the family, coached an American football team. In October 1916 the battalion was moved to Hill 60 sector on the Ypres Salient and by 1917 the Germans had captured the high ground there.

The soldiers regularly took part in raids to the enemy camp and crater fighting, leading up to the Battle of Messines in June 1917. During this time the soldiers had to dig out new trenches and raided the enemy for ammunition and supplies.[1] Sydney's stick grenade throwing skills were key to these raids. During a raid in early February 1917 Sydney was blown up with other members of his unit. He was dragged into a trench and ended up lying under the bodies of others who had tried to help him for about thirty-six hours; eventually he was rescued by some of his friends.

Two types of courage

In 1992 a group of amateur archaeologists found the remains of an original British trench in Ypres. In addition to the hundreds of artefacts they also found the remains of 155 soldiers from both sides of the conflict. The trench system and its story were featured in the BBC documentary *The Forgotten Battlefield*. The soldiers' remains received an appropriate burial by the Commonwealth War Graves Commission. Only one soldier could be identified from his dog-tag: a French soldier called François Metzinger. He died on 21 May 1915 and his body had lain undiscovered through the second and third Battles of Ypres. I cannot find words to describe the horror of the trench system. In the BBC documentary the reconstructed trenches are supported by new wooden beams and walkways. Sydney lay among the mud and blood of Ypres, his own life seeping into these graves of human flesh and blood. It seems he was only found when he was heard calling Nellie's name.

Back in London, approximately 170 miles away from Belgium and France, Nellie had a vision of Sydney calling her name. She knew that God wanted her to look for him. She knew he was injured and needed her. Nellie spoke to her father who believed her vision and helped her to secure her passage to France. Her plan was to try to get onto a warship travelling across the English Channel. She had to pester the War Office to allow her to go, even claiming: "I can cook on a troop ship." Nellie was so convinced that she had to find Sydney that she said goodbye to their daughter, Connie, who was just eighteen months old. Bravery in uncertain times means not knowing what you will find ahead of you, yet knowing that you have to act, no matter what the cost may be.

While these events were unfolding in London, Sydney received basic medical care at the aid post situated close to this trench near the front line. He had extensive injuries, having lost an eye and a leg due to multiple shrapnel wounds. His grandson (our friend, Richard) can still remember the scarring on Sydney's arms from the shrapnel. Sydney was carried by a relay of men who themselves were at risk simply by taking him to safety. To give some idea of the size of the battlefield and the lethal hail of death that rained down: an iron harvest of 160 tonnes of munitions from bullets, stick grenades, and naval gun shells was removed from the fields in Ypres in 2012.[2]

The pain Sydney experienced must have been horrific; he would have felt each bump on the long journey home. Eventually his wounds were dressed in the dressing station which would have still been part of the trench network – a simple dugout manned by the men of the Royal Army Medical Corps. These dressing stations could deal with up to 2,000 casualties a week.

Sydney's brigade was supported by the 4th Field Ambulance Service but it is likely that he was taken to the advanced dressing station at Hooge Chateau and then out of the battlefield area past Dickebusch and on to a clearing hospital several miles behind the trenches either by this mode of transport or by motorized lorry. The clearing hospital would have been a large static medical facility where supplies were scarce. One also has to remember that mud-filled wounds were breeding grounds for infection. And the infection hosts were exhausted young men with little resilience who were probably malnourished and suffering from body lice and trench foot. Let's remember too that penicillin did not enter use until 1945. The scale of some of these injuries had not been seen before and the stretched men and women caring for these soldiers were learning on the job, treating as many as 1,000 men at a time. A hundred years on and it is now possible to visit the war cemeteries at the site of these clearing stations. One example is Lijssenthoek, the location of a field hospital near Ypres. Unlike some of the larger cemeteries, all the graves there carry personal details because those buried were known to the hospital team.

There was also a Belgian military hospital in Hoogestadt staffed by British nurses and doctors, situated seven or eight miles south of Furnes on the Ypres road. One of the nurses who worked there described it after the second battle of Ypres: "Our hospital soon became a shambles, the theatre a slaughter house."[3] It was in such appalling conditions as these that Sydney ended up lying in a mess of muddied sheets in the gap between life and death in a field hospital, and where Nellie found him, still streaked with mud from what he thought was his last resting place.

After the casualty clearing hospital the soldiers were transported to a base hospital by ambulance, train, or by barge along the canal system. The further away these men were removed from the world of mud and tunnels, the more likely they were to survive. The main hospitals were at Boulogne, Rouen, Le Touquet, and Etaples – all close to ports. The men travelling to them were often called "Blighty cases" – having received wounds that were not absolutely life-threatening but bad enough to have them sent home. Nellie travelled with Sydney.

After several months they found themselves in a convoy of three hospital ships bringing the wounded soldiers back home. The main disembarkation points in the UK were Southampton and Dover. Dover alone dealt with 1,260,506 casualties during World War I. The hospital ships were covered by Article Four of the Hague Convention of 1907 but the Imperial German Navy still ordered its submarines to attack these mercy ships. This was a time of unrestricted warfare as the Germans attacked Allied shipping lanes and deliberately targeted the hospital ships. Twelve British hospital ships were sunk during World War I, two of which were the other boats in Nellie and Sydney's convoy.

On 6 April 1917 the United States entered the war. President Woodrow Wilson gave as the reason the unrestricted submarine warfare introduced by the Germans in his speech to Congress. He said: "Even hospital ships and ships carrying relief to the sorely bereaved and stricken people of Belgium… have been sunk with a reckless lack of compassion or principle."

For the families waiting for news this was a difficult time. Both the torpedoed vessels were carrying men named S. Clarke. After the stressful journey back home Sydney had to spend two years in a hospital in Brighton and then in Queen Mary's Convalescent Hospital, Roehampton, for rehabilitation and limb fitting. The family initially lived permanently in Brighton so they could visit him until he moved to Roehampton. When Sydney eventually came home he found that money was so tight that Nellie had used his cricket whites to make clothes for their daughter. Their lives looked so different from when they married in 1913. With help from family they bought a house and rented out two of the three floors for income.

Sydney and his friends built a summer house in the garden so he could watch the cricket.

On 25 August 1942 Nellie died, following a battle with leukaemia. It is an amazing story of a woman who faced great uncertainty with extraordinary courage; a woman who left her young daughter behind to travel across war-torn Europe in an effort to find the man she loved. Her legacy impacted many in her family. Her own daughter went on to work for the Women's Voluntary Service (WVS) and cared for wounded Gurkha soldiers after World War II.

Bravery in the everyday

I doubt many of us will be in the position of crossing war-torn Europe to find the man or woman we love. How can we understand the pain and the misery of Flanders fields? Would you be able to hear the quiet voice of God speaking to you through the clamour of war? At the start of the second Battle of Ypres the shelling of the German trenches was said to be so loud that it could be heard in England, and even as far away as Dublin.

If you walk through your local graveyard you will pass headstones from one hundred years ago with names like Nellie, Mabel, or Elizabeth; Stephen, Norman, or Sydney. These names are the marks on stones embedded in life's soil of people who showed extraordinary bravery in uncertain times. If I turn to my Bible I find Esther, Ruth, Nehemiah, Daniel, and Samson, to name but a few, who lived through Israel's turbulent times but showed immense bravery, standing up to declare faith or take the right course of action. Esther stood up for her faith and people in the royal court of a foreign land. Ruth followed her mother-in-law into a new country, culture, and faith despite walking the path of grief. Nehemiah returned to the forgotten words of the Law. Many of his people had even forgotten their own native language because they had been totally assimilated into the surrounding culture. He dreamed the impossible of rebuilding Jerusalem and dared to ask King Artaxerxes for permission to go and oversee the work. Daniel believed in the prophet's promise of a return from exile. Samson's life was dedicated to God and blessed in strength but he let lust blind him. He gave his life to serve God and wage war on the Philistines. Nellie travelled across France to the bloodied fields of Flanders to find her husband. Bravery in uncertain times.

Prayer

Father,

We live in uncertain times. We can watch the news and be overcome by world events. There are so many wars and signs of trouble.

Help us to keep rooted in You. Help us to remember that we can trust You. You are the end and the beginning. You never change.

In Jesus' name,

Amen.

CHAPTER 8

FACING UP TO FORGIVENESS

One of the hardest things we can do is forgive people. In this chapter we will look at the example of Jesus. We will discuss the cost of making the right and brave decision: forgiving and knowing you have been hurt but being brave and knowing that it won't define you.

I have loved the TV drama *Dr Foster* written by Mike Bartlett and produced by the BBC. It stars Suranne Jones who plays Dr Gemma Foster. In the programme Dr Foster's wonderful life starts falling apart as she discovers her husband has had an affair. Through series one and two I have really been challenged about forgiveness. How big is our forgiveness?

One of the most iconic images of the last century was the photo called "Girl in the picture". The photo, taken on 8 June 1972, is of children fleeing a napalm attack during the Vietnam War. The children pictured lived in the village of Trang Bang and had been heading to safety to a South Vietnamese position as their village was bombed. Enemy aircraft mistook the group for soldiers and bombed them. The terrified girl in the photo is Phan Thi Kim Phuc who was nine years old at the time. The famous photo was taken by Associated Press photographer, Nick Ut, and shows the little girl running from the attack with no clothes on and severe burns on her back. Shortly after the photograph she was taken to hospital. Nick Ut's photo was on the front of the *New York Times* the next day and went on to win a Pulitzer Prize and the award for World Press Photo of the Year. Kim ended up in the Barsky Hospital, an American hospital in Saigon, for fourteen months and underwent a total of seventeen skin grafts.

In 2008 Kim Phuc said: "Forgiveness made me free from hatred. I still have many scars on my body and severe pain most days but my heart is cleansed."[1] In 1982 Kim Phuc converted to Christianity. She went on to study medicine in Vietnam and Cuba. Then, in 1992, while on honeymoon, Kim Phuc and her husband were able to seek asylum as their plane touched down to refuel in Newfoundland, Canada. She is now a citizen of Canada where she and her husband established the Kim Phuc Foundation providing medical and psychological support to children affected by war. Kim still carries the scars of that day in 1972 and has gone on to have laser surgery for the scarring on her arms. Her story is an amazing one of bravery in forgiveness. She was able to forgive the North Vietnamese army that killed her cousins and left her badly burned.

Psychologists define forgiveness as a conscious decision to release feelings of resentment. This can be towards a person, a group of people, or an organization. It certainly leads to inner peace as the victim learns to release these feelings of resentment but it does not mean that everything is washed away. Like

Kim Phuc, we are left with the scars. As a Christian, I believe that we can be empowered by God to release the pain of the hurt without letting it define us.

Steps to forgiveness

Dr Fred Luskin is known as a "forgiveness expert" or a pioneer in the science and practice of forgiveness. He is also the director of Stanford University Forgiveness Project. In an article published in 2010 he acknowledges that forgiveness is a difficult concept.[2] He suggests that forgiveness is close to grief and that as with grief, if we do not process it effectively, we are left with lifelong problems. Having gone through multiple episodes of grief, I am unsure how I feel about forgiveness being close to grief but I do agree that we cannot leave it swept under a carpet of brain cells in our mind. Luskin does, however, suggest that there are steps towards forgiveness, just as there are steps to grief.

The first step towards being ready to forgive is to acknowledge that we do more harm to our self if we do not forgive those who have hurt us. The next step is to acknowledge all the emotions associated with the event. As in grief we need to express how we feel. This is certainly something we are not culturally good at in the UK or in the Northern Hemisphere. As we experience these emotions we allow our self to let go of them. We have all heard stories of great atrocities during war. For many of these victims it is only in unearthing the truth that they are fully able to forgive. It means exposing the raw emotions of the experience, rather akin to opening new wounds.

In my branch of nursing we deal with a lot of wounds. Some wounds are simple lacerations, while others are deep wounds that need time to heal. If a patient had a deep wound or an abscess I would not simply cover it with a dry dressing that I would use for a simple laceration. A minor cut heals by primary intention as the two edges of the wound are helped to meet or knit together.

Healing by secondary intention is used for deeper wounds. The wound is often extensive and there may even be some tissue loss. The edges cannot be brought together. They take longer to heal, the scarring is greater, and so is the risk of complications such as infection. The deeper the hurt and the more extensive the assault, the longer we need to allow for the healing process to occur.

In some instances I would clean the wound, wash it out, and pack it with something that will encourage healing from the depths of the wound. If I just covered it over, the top layer of the wound might heal but would leave a sinus or a cavity underneath. This can then fill with pus and infection, causing more problems in the future. The top layer would need to be opened up again to enable the wound to heal properly. Some wounds may need to be left open to allow drainage. We too need to deal with each episode of unforgiveness even though we may not have deserved the assault.

The final step, according to Luskin, is that we should be open and honest about the experience. I agree that these are crucial steps towards forgiveness but many of us find ourselves stuck at that step. We have started the journey of forgiveness and have got out onto the platform at this point but are not ready to go where the next train may take us.

Just as with truth and reconciliation, we have to face the emotion and truth of what has happened and then move forward. Here is Archbishop Desmond Tutu, writing about forgiveness: "True reconciliation is based on forgiveness, and forgiveness is based on true confession, and confession is based on penitence, on contrition, on sorrow for what you have done."[3] He learned these truths from his faith and working as the chairman of the Truth and Reconciliation Commission in South Africa in the post-apartheid era.

I have to admit that I am slow at saying sorry but if I have an argument with my husband then one of us has to be ready to say "I am sorry". When we hurt people we need to be humble enough to confess our sin. God's simple promise in Psalm 51:17 reminds us: "A broken and contrite heart [I] will not despise."

Confession has for years been considered to be one of the spiritual disciplines. It is the sharing of our deepest failures and weaknesses with God our Father. Sometimes that may also include sharing them with someone you trust or your accountability group. According to 1 John 1:9 "If we confess our sins, he who is faithful and just will forgive us our sins and cleanse us from all unrighteousness" (*Life with God Bible*).

Forgiveness in the Bible

God's journey with the nation of Israel teaches us about our forgiving God. Reading through some of the books of the Old Testament such as Leviticus and Numbers can be overwhelming in many ways but they teach us so much about love and true forgiveness. Love is mentioned for the first time in the Bible in the book of Leviticus, the book of law. Probably compiled by Moses as his farewell address, it teaches about the overwhelming presence of God and how He was truly present with His people if they followed Him.

Right at the start of the book Moses is summoned by God to the tent of meeting and we are reminded that these words are divine revelation. As read through Leviticus I have to stop and pause as there is provision made for forgiveness of all people, from the lowly peasant up to priests and even kings. God knew His people would make mistakes and would not be able to follow His prescriptions for holy living.

In Leviticus 1–4 we learn about all the offerings that can be given for redemption of sin. What amazes me is that God forgives although we don't deserve it. He accepts the whole burnt offering of a bull, a male without blemish. The forgiveness described in Leviticus 1 for this sacrifice is mirrored in 1 John 1:5–10. And for those who could not afford a livestock offering God made provision, allowing His people to sacrifice turtle doves or a common pigeon. Again and again God forgives His people as they turn back to Him and confess their wrongdoing. In the book of Hosea God illustrates this, comparing Israel to an unfaithful wife, divorcing her yet loving her and accepting her back.

Ultimately, God had to send Jesus as the final sacrifice for our sin. We were never going to pay that price ourselves. Jesus was always God's perfect plan.

Hebrews 10:14 in *The Message* puts it clearly: "It was a perfect sacrifice by a perfect person to perfect some very imperfect people. By that single offering, he did everything that needed to be done for everyone who takes part in the purifying process."

This is challenging when we consider the cost of God's forgiveness to us and yet we struggle with forgiveness ourselves. We wonder how we can forgive and are reminded of Jesus' words while dying for us: "Father, forgive them, for they know not what they do" (Luke 23:34, ESV).

There are times when trying to forgive seems an impossible task. Forgiveness should start with God. His Holy Spirit convicts us of our wrongdoing. We may not be able to forget but we can start to forgive others or ourselves through the strength God gives us. By forgiving, we are brave enough to accept the reality of what has happened and to find resolution in God's presence.

Forgiveness is vital. Jesus shows us how important it is by placing it at the heart of the prayer he teaches his disciples in Matthew 6:

> "This, then, is how you should pray:
>
> 'Our Father in heaven,
> hallowed be your name,
> your kingdom come,
> your will be done,
> on earth as it is in heaven.
> Give us today our daily bread.
> And forgive us our debts,
> as we also have forgiven our debtors.
> And lead us not into temptation,
> but deliver us from the evil one.'"

We are reminded as we pray that God has forgiven us, so how can we not forgive others? God loves us with an unending love. He holds us in the palm of His hand. We are reminded to love him with all our heart, mind, and strength. That includes making the decision to forgive others no matter how they have hurt us, as we too are sinners. We too can never get everything right. We too will fail.

There are also times when the person we need to forgive does not want to accept our forgiveness. They either do not think they have done anything wrong or just can't accept it. I know that I have hurt others, asked their forgiveness, and they have not responded. I am so glad that God shields me from the pain this could cause me. I know He forgives me as He looks at me and sees Jesus. It is up to each of us to move on and not to be stuck in the past, but we also have to be realistic in our expectations of others. If we have really hurt someone we may need to give them time. They may move to the point of forgiveness but it can take a while. They may not be able to forgive today but they may be able to forgive tomorrow.

We also need to remember that to forgive someone does not automatically mean that we will be reconciled. I was chatting about this to Malcolm who has worked for many years in the field of reconciliation. His response was that reconciliation is bilateral; forgiveness can often be unilateral. The important point to remember is that we have to allow God to do this work in us. Kim Phuc found true forgiveness only when she came to know Jesus.

Prayer

Father,

There are times when I struggle to forgive those who hurt me.

Help me to be brave and take the first step. Remind me of Your Son and how He has forgiven me.

Strengthen me through Your spirit to do as Jesus would do.

If it means opening old wounds then allow Your Spirit to minister into them, cleaning out the debris so that I can heal in Your way.

I know that I am not perfect, only You are. Help me to also be able to forgive myself as well as those who have hurt me. Help me to love as Jesus loves.

In Jesus' name.

Amen.

CHAPTER 9

QUIETNESS CAN BE BRAVE!

In this chapter we are going to look at the idea that even in quiet ways we be brave. This is not the typical picture we imagine when we think of bravery and brave people. We may think of David wrestling with a lion or people running into burning buildings to rescue people. There are people who we know that have never been awarded the George Cross but have bravely lived the life they were called to.

Sometimes I cannot sleep. I mean I *really* cannot sleep. I toss and turn, try to do relaxation techniques, and then I quietly head downstairs to have a mug of hot milk and read for a while. The other night I was up until 4 a.m. and it was interesting looking out into the street. For a short while, between the night-time revellers at the local pub and the early morning commuters on the way to work, there is silence (although not complete silence as you can occasionally hear the distinctive sound of a fox).

At moments like these I have started reading about the lives of some of the great saints of the church: words to feed the spirit and soul. I recently read this prayer by St Basil. My friends Barbara and Eric sent it to me after we had been discussing being brave in the light of uncertainty.

Eric commented: "The prayer imagines our life journey as the voyage of a ship. It seems to me that 'bravely' could be appropriately inserted into the prayer as I have done below."

SHOW ME THE COURSE

> Steer the ship of my life, good Lord,
> To your quiet harbour,
> Where I can be safe from the storms
> of sin and conflict.
> Show me the course I should take.
> Renew in me the gift of discernment,
> So that I can always see
> the right direction to take.
> And give me the strength and the courage
> To [bravely] choose the right course,
> Even when the sea is rough
> And the waves are high,
> Knowing that through
> enduring hardship and danger
> in your name
> I shall find comfort and peace.[1]

I loved the prayer when I read it, and then I started reading about St Basil's life. I had not appreciated how much his life has impacted the wider church family that I love and am a part of today.

Basil was fortunate to be born the son of a wealthy family in Cappadocia, modern-day Turkey, in about 330 AD. Not only were his family wealthy in money but also in spiritual heritage; his father, known as Basil the Elder, was a Christian. In fact, his maternal grandfather was a Christian martyr, executed in the years prior to Emperor Constantine's conversion. Basil's father was a well-known lawyer and rhetorician. His mother and father were both known for their goodness and righteousness, bringing up nine children, five of whom are remembered by name and venerated as saints: Basil the Great, Gregory of Nyssa, Peter of Sebaste, Naucratius, and Saint Macrina the Younger.[2] His parents lived their lives to glorify God in quiet ways, not to stand out in a crowd.

These qualities are also seen in Basil. He was fortunate enough to receive a good education. During that time he became a lifelong friend of Gregory of Nazianzus, known as the "Trinitarian Theologian" and whose work still impacts theology today. At that time Basil worked as a lawyer and it was not until several years later, after Basil met a charismatic bishop known as Eustathius of Sebaste, that he felt he had woken up from a deep sleep. Drawn into communal religious life, by 358 AD Basil was gathering around him a group of like-minded friends and family. In 360 AD Basil attended the Council of Constantinople. He initially sided with his friend Eustathius, who refused to support the Nicene Creed; however, Basil eventually abandoned this stance and later became a firm advocate of it. In later life he battled with those who spread Arianism – the belief that states that although Jesus Christ is the Son of God, He is distinct from and therefore subordinate to the Father. Through the way he lived, Basil's example brought about a change in monastic practice, moving it away from its former harshness to a greater balance between service and prayer. Not only is he remembered as the father of Eastern monasticism, his legacy extends also to the Western church due to his impact on St Benedict. As recently as 2008, Pope Benedict XVI asserted that

St Benedict's life and work had had a fundamental influence on the development of European civilization and culture and helped Europe to emerge from Roman rule.[3]

I can guarantee that St Basil never expected his life would have such a profound impact on the world around him and for many centuries to come.

St Basil of Caesarea, also called St Basil the Great, has a day named after him (1 January) as well as numerous churches and cathedrals. He was without doubt an influential theologian and eventually became one of the Nicene Creed's strongest supporters. He was opposed to the heresies of the early Christian church, standing his ground against both Arianism and the followers of Apollinaris of Laodicea. Much like his parents and grandparents, he was known for his care of the poor and his virtuous life. I have no hesitation in calling him brave. He was courageous for a season when the church needed him to be. He displayed bravery in quiet ways as he steered monasticism towards service and prayer.

Brave in the everyday

There are many people like that who have never had a book published, or appeared on TV, or even in a YouTube clip. They too have lived lives that show bravery in quiet ways, impacting the communities they live in. These people are living out the Christ life in a Christ way. I feel that, as a Christian community, we have failed to communicate the value of working in a non-glamorous nine-to-five job, being stay-at-home parents or carers. Most of us don't think we have a vivid colourful life that stands out.

We need to shout from the rooftops of our churches: Don't be ashamed of what you think is your quiet or small life. Keep serving God. Use your life to glorify God by loving others, helping the oppressed, serving the poor, and dealing with injustice. Use your life to speak words of love and truth to others.

We cannot all be like Malala Yousafzai (the young Pakistani girl who was shot by the Taliban for promoting education for girls) or a firefighter rushing into a burning building. Just be you. Remember that courage is bravery for a season. It consists of the small, daily acts of bravery. It can also become a habit like a muscle you regularly exercise.

A few years ago I was off work recuperating from major surgery. I could not get out and about as I was temporarily unable to drive and was so dependent on others. In fact I felt pretty useless. I was receiving only statutory sick pay and was worried about how we would cope financially. To make ends meet I decided to sell some items online. While browsing I found someone selling a bundle of branded girls' clothes that I knew would be worth getting. I know… I should not have looked! The lady I bought them from sent me a message asking for feedback. When the clothes arrived they were not what I thought they would be, and so I let the lady know. Instead of apologizing as I thought she would I received a long reply about how her husband had left her and how life was so difficult. She was struggling to cope with two small children. I simply replied: "I am a Christian and believe prayer changes things. God is interested in you."

Initially there was silence but several weeks later I received her reply. It was a Sunday night and I was online instead of resting. The hairs rose on the back of my neck and arms as I read her response. She wrote and told me that my message had stopped her ending her life. She had never thought God was interested in her. She went on to say that she was improving and that life did not seem so bleak. I was stunned.

I am still stunned today. I am not telling you this story to make you think I am a really spiritual person. The truth is rather that I do not think I had really thought about what I had written. God used what I had said to change her life. It still makes me cry today.

I thought I was living a quiet life but the message from Heaven was loud and clear. Your words and actions speak volumes. They resonate around your home, your community, and the world. Allow God to direct them and you can be the touchpaper for change or the person who creates a huge impact in the most complex of situations.

In the 1920s, the German-American geologist Walter H. Bucher studied a number of crater sites (now called impact craters) in the United States. His studies suggested that this unique geological structure was created by some great explosive, most likely a volcano. Then, in 1936, the geologists John D. Boon and Claude C. Albritton Jr proved that the craters that Bucher studied were probably formed by impact events rather than volcanos. An impact crater is usually a circular depression in the surface of a planet or moon formed by the hypervelocity impact of a smaller body. The high-speed object produces shock waves so both the projectile object and the immobile object are compressed, ultimately leading to an explosion. An impact crater is created by a much smaller object. To see examples all we have to do is look closely at the surface of the moon.

On the morning of 30 June 1908 there was an explosion in the Tunguska region of Eastern Siberia which flattened 2,000 sq km of forest. Thankfully there were no human casualties as it was then, and remains now, one of the least habitable areas in Siberia. The explosion is believed to be due to the air burst of a meteoroid and was classified as an impact event even though no impact crater was evident. The Tunguska event is the largest impact event in Earth's recorded history.

Sometimes the smallest objects can cause the largest impact and often we can be totally unaware of the triggering event. In the economy of God, a kind word, an outstretched arm, a small act of generous living can be divinely accelerated to create an impact that is the equivalent of the Tunguska event in Siberia or the Rio Cuarto crater field in Argentina. Years later we may discover what happened but for now only God knows the chain of events.

Quietness in the Bible

In point of fact we are all called to live a quiet life. We should make it our ambition – to lead a quiet life. The Living Bible paraphrase of Paul's words in 1 Thessalonians 4:11 puts it this way: "This should be your ambition: to live a quiet life, minding your own business and doing your own work, just as we told you before."

The Christians in Thessalonica had been accused of stirring up discontent in the church[4] so Paul encourages them to continue living to please God by pursuing a holy life and loving others. Paul is suggesting that we should all lead a peaceful and tranquil life, striving to seek a peaceful life without conflict with our community. This idea of a "quiet life" might initially appear to be at odds with Jesus' own words telling us to "go and tell" in Matthew 26:16–20. I think that Paul is talking about a "quiet life" as an attitude rather than a physical state of being. This means that we should still be speaking out against injustices and proclaiming the gospel but out of an attitude that reflects a quiet inner life. It is a challenging call but one that we can all act on if we allow God to encourage us to be brave.

There are so many people who have lived the life they felt called to do and we will never know what they did. Their lives may have touched a generation. There will be times when you will never know the impact of actions and words as their story has been hidden by the weight of history. I am reminded of Nicholas Winton who was a British humanitarian. He organized the rescue of 669 Jewish children from Czechoslovakia to Britain during World War Two in an operation later known as the Czech *Kindertransport*. What he did was hidden for nearly fifty years. In 2003 he was knighted by the queen for his service to humanity.

After the war Nicholas Winton worked for the International Refugee Organisation and the International Bank for Reconstruction and Development in Paris. He met his wife Grete there and married her in 1948. Eventually they moved to Maidenhead, England. Although he did talk about what he did during the war it was not until 1988 that his wife Grete found his detailed notebooks which contained the list of children's names and family details that he saved. Then, in 1988, the BBC broadcast a special episode of *That's Life* when Winton was invited to the show. You can see clips of what happened on YouTube. The host of the show, Esther Rantzen, asked the audience if anyone owed their lives to Nicholas Winton and more than a dozen people stood and applauded him. In October 2016 I visited Prague and saw a memorial to what he did, which included photos of the children he saved. Each display shared photos and the story of what the children did as they grew up. A remarkable story about a man who simply did what he felt was right.

Last year (2017) was the 500th anniversary of the publication of Martin Luther's Ninety-five Theses. Toy company Playmobil manufactured a figure of Martin Luther to celebrate this event. Marin Luther was a German professor of theology, priest, and monk, and a seminal figure in the Reformation. His figure has become one of the fastest-selling in history, outstripping even the Star Wars figures. I have to confess that I was one of the people who bought one. I actually bought it for my husband and it sits on his desk.

The great reformer Martin Luther is said to have nailed his Theses to the door of the church in Wittenburg Castle where he had worked. It is unclear as to whether he did actually nail them there. The more important aspect of the story is that these Theses were published and reached the eyes and ears of people who read the objections and shouted for change. The Theses laid out the objectives to the injustices within the Roman Catholic Church, particularly the selling of indulgences as a way of securing less time in purgatory (the space between Heaven and hell).

Luther is said to have been inspired by John Wycliffe, who challenged the opulence of the church and is said to have translated the Bible into English, making it available to the people in 1382. There are so many other people who we know influenced Luther – from Desiderius Erasmus' publication of the Greek New Testament in 1516 to the Czech priest Jan Hus who was burned at the stake in 1514 for his passion to see reform in the Roman Catholic church.

Marguerite de Navarre was the older sister of King Francis I of France. She became one of the most educated women in France – an able diplomat who supported the voices of the Reformation and who is said to have hidden John Calvin as he fled from Paris to Geneva in 1533. Or there is Argula von Grumbach, a noblewoman from Bulgaria, famous for writing to Ingolstadt University in 1523, supporting one of its students who was persecuted for his Lutheran views. She was able to voice this injustice and people listened to her. Other women who stood up with conviction are Olympia Morata who, by the age of twelve, was able to converse fluently in Greek and Latin. She became a mentor to many in the court and also lectured on Cicero and Calvin's works. Or what about Jean of Albret who is known as the spiritual and political leader of the French Huguenot movement?

Sometimes what we do is not always recognized. It is with hindsight that we can look back and see the craters in our midst. Or what we do may only be recognized after we are gone. It may never be recognized. God alone may see the labours of our hands and heart. We are called to run this race compelled by the love of God. We are called to do what God wants us to do.

Prayer

Father,

Thank you that we come in all shapes and sizes. Thank you that we have a variety of personalities and giftings. Use us where we are. Help us to listen to You. Guide us how to serve You best.

Help us to be brave, to have the courage for wherever we are on our journeys in life.

And give us the strength and the courage to bravely choose the right path in life even when the ground is rough.

In Jesus' name.

Amen.

CHAPTER 10

COPING WITH GRIEF AND LOSS

I hesitated before I agreed to write this chapter. It's not a coincidence that it is towards the end of the book. It is one that I did not want to step into, having been in this place a lot in the last three years. Loss seems to be a much more common occurrence in my life, but I do know that understanding the nature of grief helps us cope with loss. So I have split this chapter in two. The first part is predominately about grief, and the second about loss.

Bravery through grief

Grief is hard to talk about. I think this is because grief also begets grief. I have learned that you can attend a funeral and feel quite together but all the grief you have experienced in the past can bubble up under the surface. Emotions that are linked to loss can be triggered throughout our lives from anniversaries, other key dates, or a visit to a familiar place. You never get over loss. As time passes, the intensity of feeling of loss will lessen but you cannot erase an emotional memory. It leaves a scar that you have for life. The old English word for grief is "heartsarnes" and it literally translates as "heart soreness". Your heart is scarred.

I once wrote a children's story called *Waves*. It was about a little boy who lost his mother. At the end of the story he was standing by the sea with his grandfather. His grandfather told him that the waves were the same as the sadness he was experiencing. At first the feelings of grief are like the huge waves that roll in and catch you unawares. Slowly over time they get less and less but can still touch you when you don't expect them. I feel like I have stood at the water's edge quite a few times but I know that I am not standing there by myself.

Grief is a natural, and surprisingly healthy process that enables us to recover from the deep, deep emotions we experience when we lose someone. While grief is an expected response to such a significant loss the unfamiliar emotions that arise after death are often new. They can make us feel helpless, fearful, and even isolated from the world. And each person's journey is different with ups and downs. There may be moments of quiet followed by moments of anguish that can hit you as strong waves of emotion. The first few days after someone dies are generally the most intense. There is chaos as you have strong emotions that you may never have felt before. Over the following days emotions from guilt to anger or despair may creep up on you. It is so hard to describe.

Grief is also associated with physical, as well as mental, pain. C. S. Lewis, in his book, *A Grief Observed*, likened bereavement to a feeling of being "mildly drunk or concussed". There is a range of physical manifestations of grief. I have discussed these in my previous book: *The Art of Daily Resilience.*[1] Here are just a few:

- general fatigue

- random pains and aches

- an inability to sit still, restlessness

- gastric distress, such as an ulcer, inflammation of the esophagus, or colitis

- breathlessness/shortness of breath

- heart palpitations

- loss of appetite or its opposite: comfort eating

- insomnia

- muscle weakness

- increased blood pressure (also an increased risk of heart attack and blood clots)

- anxiety attacks

- suppressed immune system.

There are so many ways to describe grief. Some describe it as being in a boat on a stormy sea; others may describe it as a roller coaster journey with all the ups and downs. When we first experience grief we are launched into a huge tempest of emotions. We may feel we are surrounded by darkness and heavy waves of sadness. Any comforting words from friends and family are drowned out by the howling winds of sorrow. There are also as many theories about grief as there are illustrations.

Theories of grief

It may be surprising to hear that Sigmund Freud pioneered the study of mourning. It is only really in the last forty odd years that bereavement research has gained any real prominence in psychology. One such researcher was the aforementioned well-known Swiss-American psychiatrist Dr Elisabeth Kübler-Ross. She was a pioneer in near-death studies and the author of the groundbreaking book *On Death and Dying*. In the book she first discussed her theory of the five stages of grief and popularized this model of grieving based upon her research into how terminally ill persons respond to the news of their terminal illness.

Dr Kübler-Ross suggested that death should be considered a normal stage of life. She offered strategies for treating patients and their families as they negotiate the five stages of grief. Many like this model as it has a simple linear approach. Since its publication, this stage model has also been applied to other losses such as divorce, long-term conditions, and infertility.

The stages of grief are as follows:

1. *Denial*: This is the shock reaction.

2. *Anger*: Resentment grows. We ask, "Why me?" or "Why my...?"

3. *Bargaining*: We try to make a deal, insisting that things be the way they used to be.

4. *Depression*: Now we say, "Yes, me." The courage to admit our loss brings sadness (which can be healthy mourning

and grieving) and/or hopelessness (which is unhealthy mourning and grieving).

5. *Acceptance*: Now we face our loss calmly. It is a time of reflection and possible regrouping.

Much of the earlier work on the stages of grief are attributed to Bowlby and Parkes. The psychoanalyst Bowlby studied early attachment and primary relationships.[2] From these studies he suggests that grief is a predictable orderly pattern of response to a death. Colin Murray Parkes, however, suggests that grieving is a process, a sequence of reactions to the death of a significant loved one. Parkes suggested a phase theory of how the bereaved return to feelings of safety and security again as they resolve their grief. His focus was very much on how people process information, and he proposed that the bereaved filter out unwanted information to help them return to normal.[3] Parkes argued that the bereaved must progress through four overlapping phases of grief before the process of realization is complete:

- The first, which can be called shock and numbness, is when individuals have difficulty comprehending and believing that the death has occurred.

- In the second phase, also known as yearning and searching, they may refuse to acknowledge the loss and attempt to return things to the way they were. This is almost a pre-loss stage.

- In the third stage they realize that this is not possible and often feel frustration; anger may result. This can be called disorganization and despair as the person becomes easily distracted and has trouble focusing.

• In the fourth phase of reorganization and recovery the individual realizes that life continues without the deceased and begins to rebuild life without them.

Many of these models of grief and bereavement follow a pattern or order. Personally I think grief is not linear. I think you can dip in and out of the different phases. Sometimes that may be several times in one day. I would therefore describe grief as a messy picture of different colours with each colour expressing a different emotion.

Writer Molly Fumia describes grief as "a journey, often perilous and without clear direction".[4] She suggests that the experience of grieving cannot be ordered or categorized, hurried or controlled, pushed aside or ignored indefinitely.

Dr Bob Kellemen is the Vice President for Institutional Development, Chair of the Biblical Counselling Department at Crossroads Bible College, and the Founder and CEO of RPM Ministries. He proposes a biblical approach to grieving. He suggests that there are eight scriptural "stages" in our responses to life's losses.[5] He calls his description of moving through hurt to hope in Christ – from grieving to growing – "Biblical Sufferology". He also reminds us that these stages are a relational process and are not in sequential steps as grieving and growing are messy.

Stages	Typical relief response	Biblical grief
Stage 1	Denial/isolation	Candour: honesty with self
Stage 2	Anger/resentment	Complaint: honesty with God
Stage 3	Bargaining/works	Cry: asking God for help
Stage 4	Depression/alienation	Comfort: receiving God's help
Stage 5	Regrouping	Waiting: trusting with faith
Stage 6	Deadening	Wailing: groaning with hope
Stage 7	Despairing/doubting	Weaving: perceiving with grace
Stage 8	Digging cisterns	Worshipping: engaging with love

A model of "Biblical Sufferology"

I want to remind us that it's also good and right to grieve. It is a natural process. I think we can also find spiritual encouragement as we become more aware of life's inevitable sadness and pain. Without the pain and sorrow of grief we do not appreciate the opposite of it. There is also a dichotomy with grief as we live with grief and trust. Grief leads to a sense of loss of control. It also leads us to trust God more. It enables us to be honest about our sadness and pain. We know that death is tragic; death is sorrowful. It does not matter how the person died or what age they are, they have died and we will not see them for a while.

Recently I was speaking at Spring Harvest. Just half an hour before my session my great aunty died. I knew that I would not be at my best. I started the session by explaining that I had just had some sad news and not to ask me how old she was. Does the age of a person matter? The grief is real. The pain is still there.

We do, however, have hope. As Christians, we can *grieve temporarily*, knowing that this is only a temporal separation. It can feel more hopeless when we do not know the faith of the person who has left us. I think all we can do is trust our God. One day we will stand before Him and ask all our questions and on that day the questions will not matter.

Grief in the Bible

I think this is one of the best known Scriptures that mentions grief and mourning. It is often read out at funerals alongside Psalm 23.

Ecclesiastes 3:1–8:

> *There is a time for everything,*
> *and a season for every activity under the heavens:*
> *a time to be born and a time to die,*
> *a time to plant and a time to uproot,*
> *a time to kill and a time to heal,*
> *a time to tear down and a time to build,*
> *a time to weep and a time to laugh,*
> *a time to mourn and a time to dance,*
> *a time to scatter stones and a time to gather them,*
> *a time to embrace and a time to refrain from*
> *embracing,*
> *a time to search and a time to give up,*
> *a time to keep and a time to throw away,*
> *a time to tear and a time to mend,*
> *a time to be silent and a time to speak,*
> *a time to love and a time to hate,*
> *a time for war and a time for peace.*

Grief is an expected visitor to our lives. It is not something we can shy away from. I am not saying it's a natural response and can be easy. I cannot describe the pain and anguish you feel in grief. You have to be brave but remember that this too will pass. It turns up when we least expect it, just like the waves that roll in and hit us. We often have other plans and if you are like our family there can be times when there is little stretch for anything else. We have had two church weekends in recent years where we either could not go because someone died or someone passed away while we were there. Both incidents were completely unexpected. Thankfully we have a church family that supported us as we coped with the events that happened. They held our whole family in prayer as we negotiated heading back home.

We can openly mourn the loss of a friend or family member. We can hope for the future but we should not carry on as if nothing has happened. David, who was called a man after God's own heart, openly grieved the death of his son. There is an old expression that says, "Those who believe need not grieve." That is just not true. We may be able to grieve in hope of what is to come but the pain and anguish of grief is still as real. Your depth of grief does not imply a loss of faith.

Jesus understands this. He came and lived as a human in this broken, fractured world. He gets it – He understands. Jesus Himself experienced grief. When He saw Mary and Martha in anguish over the death of their brother Lazarus, He wept and groaned. He did not have to put Himself through it even though He knew He was about to raise Lazarus from the dead. He also knows the tormenting thirst and weakness of life's final hours.

Jesus also defeated grief. *He hates it more than we do!* Jesus broke death's power by dying and rising from the dead; He did it not only for Himself but also for all who believe in Him. Jesus promised, "Blessed are those who mourn, for they shall be comforted" (Matthew 5:4, ESV). Paul reminds us that if we have faith in Jesus then, "We do not want you to be uninformed, brothers, about those who are asleep, that you may not grieve as others do who have no hope" (1 Thessalonians 4:13, ESV). God understands. There are many stories in the Bible that show us how God comforts His people in times of sorrow and loss.

God is also with us. He is there right in the middle of the grief. The sovereign God who is above all things is also called Immanuel, which means "God *with* us". He sees you when the tears are gushing out of your eyes and run in ripples down the contours of your face. He sees you as your eyes swell up and become so sore you feel you cannot open them. He hears you as you breathe in gulps of air feeling the tight restriction of pain around your chest. He is there when you have run out of hankies and snot and tears congeal. He is there when our grief is so debilitating that it feels impossible to function: you cannot eat, drink, or sleep. He is not aloof in Heaven. He does not leave us to figure out how to handle grief on our own. He walks every step of the journey with us.

This is something the Lord does by His Spirit, through His word, prayer, and the fellowship and love of His people. Those means of grace are not things we have to do or more burdens to carry when our shoulders feel grief-weary. They are expressions of His love for us. If in the midst of your grief you struggle to pray or read the Bible then ask someone to pray for you and/or read the Bible to you. Grief is really, really hard. It hurts like nothing you have ever experienced. The Lord, however, has broken death's power. We know that He is with us and one day we will be with Him. Those who have died and trusted God will be with Him. That hope removes death's sting – it really does.

There are times when we do not know whether those who have died turned to God in their last moments. We do know, however, that God will accept them. Jesus illustrated this truth in a parable in Matthew 20:1–16. In the parable the landowner went out early in the morning and hired workers for his vineyard. He negotiated with them to pay them a fair day's wage. Later in the morning he then saw some other workers standing idle in the marketplace. He also hired them and told them that he would pay them a fair wage. Then at noon and in mid-afternoon the same thing happened. Finally, about five o'clock in the afternoon, he hired some more workers.

When the evening came he paid all the workers the same salary. The men who had worked all day grumbled because these men who had only worked one hour got the same wage that they all received after working hard all day. The landowner reminded them that he had paid them what they had agreed on. If he wanted to be generous to this last man then that was his privilege. As John Calvin remarks, "There is… no room to doubt that [Christ] is prepared to admit into his kingdom all, without exception, who shall apply to him."[6]

What can we do to help?

Watching someone go through grief will flummox the most eloquent and caring of people as they try to help. We want to say the right thing but are scared we may upset them. I have listed some helpful pointers as to what to say and how to support those going through grief. Some of the people that helped us the most were friends who stepped in and sometimes did not say a lot.

When Malcolm's dad suddenly died we were in the midst of the chaos of grief. We had four small children and had to pack and drive from Bournemouth to the ferry and cross the Irish Sea. I had to pack what we would need for a week and a funeral. Where do you start? Friends turned up, helped me pack, and handed us a bag of sandwiches, drinks, and snacks to take with us on the trip. We still remember how helpful and kind they were.

Helpful suggestions

- **No need to ask, just be a practical help.** Asking someone going through grief, "If there's anything I can do to help" is not actually helpful. Your brain does not work. You may not have the mental energy to even answer the question. You may not be able to ask for help. Think of what those in mourning may need. Do a shop and drop it off.

- **Don't tell people that you know how they feel**. You don't. No one's journey through grief is the same. You can mention having gone through something similar but express you know it's not the same.

- **Don't tell people that God is in control or that God is good.** We know these words are true but we need to be reminded of a God who is close and feels our hurts. We need to be reminded of Jesus who weeps with me, who knows my sorrow because he carried his own.

- **Be real, be honest, be patient, be kind.**

- **Don't project your ideas and beliefs on someone.** Their journey is different to yours.

- **Pray.**

This may seem to be a strange thing to say but I am grateful for having gone through this journey of grief. If I had not gone through it the colours of the world would be in monochrome. Now they resonate with deep, vibrant colours that transform my view. I also know that Jesus will be with me when I travel this road again. I know that God's perfect love casts out fear.

Prayer

Lord,

What can we say? How can we express these emotions? Sadness drips off us from every orifice. We feel only pain – no words but You know. You are with us in the grief we feel. You are one who is well acquainted with sorrow. Take these tears and water what You are doing in our lives. Help us to grow through this experience or our recollection of grief.

In Jesus' name.

Amen.

* * *

Bravery through loss

I think the biggest sense of loss I ever experienced was the loss of the job I loved. Remember I am talking here about loss, not grief.

The origin of loss is from the old English word "los" or "destruction". It has Germanic origins probably related to the

Old Norse *los* which means "breaking up of the ranks of an army".

A *loss* occurs when something is perceived to be negative by the individuals involved. It results in long-term changes in one's social situations, personal relationships, or community. The ultimate loss is considered to be the death of someone close.

Losses can be personal, such as the loss of one's vision or hearing. They can also be interpersonal, such as divorce and the loss of a marriage. You can also have a material loss such as losing a job or becoming homeless. Loss can be symbolic such as losses related to racism or a role redefinition. Then there are also intangible psychological losses that can include changes in self-worth due to a job demotion.

We can also go through traumatic or stressful events that may result in multiple losses. An example would be a person who has a long-term condition. Their partner may have to stop work and become their carer. Losses in this scenario can range from the financial, loss of physical intimacy, or an inability to do simple things together such as washing the dishes. I have not even mentioned the psychological losses, such as the loss of esteem.

My story

I was called to be a nurse as a young Christian. I remember asking God what I should do and how I should serve him. I was reading through the book of Genesis at the time and came across this verse: "Now Deborah, Rebekah's nurse".[7] It was clear to me then that I was called into nursing. I have now been a nurse for thirty years. It has been a real blessing to be part of a profession that was started by a Christian. At the heart of what we nurses do is this call to care for the whole person: body, soul, and mind.

After that call, I had a wonderful lecturer when I studied nursing in Dundee. She had been a nun and was inspirational to me; as a result I knew that one day I wanted to teach nursing too. In 2010, when we moved to the Chilterns for Malcolm to become the senior pastor at Gold Hill Baptist Church, I was offered a post as a nursing tutor at the Florence Nightingale School of Nursing, King's College London. I was thrilled. I loved it.

Then three years ago our world imploded as we experienced the tragic loss of several members of Malcolm's family. As a reaction to each death I developed pneumonia. I had already been battling the superbug MRSA in my lungs which caused me to have a chronic lung condition as well as asthma. During one time of grief, on one visit to Ireland, I became ill again. On 4 April we went to bed with sad hearts because of the grief we were experiencing, and on top of that, Malcolm had a funeral to organize. I also knew that I was deteriorating and needed to seek medical help. I got up and sat and prayed and the room was filled with a tangible presence of God. He reminded me He would be with me so I borrowed the taxi fare and headed to the Mater Hospital in Belfast. Poor Malcolm awoke the next morning to discover I was in hospital.

I was kept in for a week. It was a difficult time as I wanted to support my husband and the family. I was eventually able to return home after the hospital stay, funeral, and three weeks recuperating. I was then off work for six months.

I then went through the process of being retired on ill health grounds. It involved lots of reports, visits to occupational health and paperwork – lots of it. There was the possibility of not working again and the financial challenges of being on statutory sick pay. Going through the process of possible retirement left me bereft. I felt I was heading down the path of grief again although it was actually the sense of loss. In some sense my role and identity had become rolled into my job and where I worked. Mention King's College London and people listen to what you have to say. Not only did I love working there but I had made good friends in my workplace. I felt God challenge me about where my role and purpose came from.

I felt vulnerable. I find it difficult to explain why. Maybe I felt like my whole life was exposed as the investigators looked into my health, demanding access to GP and hospital notes, and interviewing me. I had to give it all to God – this bowl of spaghetti. It was all my feelings all mixed together. I also had to trust in God's greater plan and His will.

Doka[8] suggests this can be a negative complication in grief as people may become angry at God or just feel disempowered. I felt the opposite – trusting God meant I could stop striving. Trusting Him empowered me to cope with the loss I was feeling.

There is always a plan B, and over time my plan B became my plan A. In some amazing turnaround I ended up going back to work in a new university that was a ten-minute drive from home. I did not miss the two-hour commute into London. Some days, on the Tube, I would wake up from a doze not knowing if I was going to work or coming home. I have been able to adapt to my new role and made some amazing new friends. Some days I have to remind myself that a few years ago I could have stopped working all together.

There are so many different forms of loss. In the financial sector or financial accounting a loss is defined as an unusual decrease in net income in the business. You can also have a loss of appetite, earning, relate it to people and pets or even material possessions. You may hear of lost property offices, loss adjusters or weight loss consultants. We even use the idiom, "at a loss". The range of loss can vary from misplacing or losing a belonging to the loss of health, financial security or loved ones. Loss carries with it a sense of bewilderment or even uncertainty. Sometimes people will move from loss into the journey of grief. There isn't the depth to loss that you experience in grief but it is still a significant event. It is not one that we can race through thinking we will be completely unscathed as there is a hole where there is now a loss.

What does the Bible say about loss?

Paul reminds us that whatever we go through God's grace is enough. He reminds us of this in 2 Corinthians 12:9. We are also reminded that God will supply all our needs. Sometimes it is difficult to trust God. Think of the person who has lost their job. Yes they will have financial challenges but there are also the emotional, psychological, and physiological effects of losing a job. You may wonder who you are without a defined role or position or a timetable to the day. It can bring a real challenge around identity. Long-term unemployment has a terrible way of tearing down the structures that help us shape our identity.

The Bible reminds us that in Jesus we are allowed to see our new identity. We are chosen by God, co-heirs with Christ, children of God.

Psalm 84:6 says: "As they pass through the Valley of Baka, they make it a place of springs; the autumn rains also cover it with pools."

Psalm 23 says:

> God, my shepherd!
> I don't need a thing.
> You have bedded me down in lush meadows,
> you find me quiet pools to drink from.
> True to your word,
> you let me catch my breath
> and send me in the right direction.
>
> Even when the way goes through
> Death Valley,
> I'm not afraid
> when you walk at my side.
> Your trusty shepherd's crook
> makes me feel secure.
>
> You serve me a six-course dinner
> right in front of my enemies.
> You revive my drooping head;
> my cup brims with blessing.
>
> Your beauty and love chase after me
> every day of my life.
> I'm back home in the house of God
> for the rest of my life.[9]

Grief and loss are challenging bedfellows. They illicit a torrent of emotions. They remind us to be brave as we walk hand in hand with Jesus through the valley of weeping or Baka.

This was a valley in Palestine mentioned in Psalm 84:6 through which the exiled psalmist sees in a vision the pilgrims passing in their march towards the sanctuary of God.

Prayer

Father,

Thank you that You know exactly how I feel. You know the pain and the confusion of loss and grief. Help me to trust You, to take Your hand and walk with You through the valley of Baka.

In Jesus' name,

Amen.

CHAPTER 11

LIVING A LIFE WE DIDN'T CHOOSE

Sometimes we end up living the life we don't expect or living through what we would not have chosen for ourselves. This chapter looks at bravery when we find ourselves in these unforeseen circumstances.

I was recently on a journey from London to Uganda via Dubai, travelling with a short-term mission team. The plane had a fantastic entertainment programme. Everyone in the team was asleep but I couldn't settle. (Girls, I have the photos to prove it!) So I watched a few films and found myself watching a moving documentary.

The programme was called, *A Time to Die, A Time to Live*, taken from the passage we have already mentioned in Ecclesiastes chapter 3. On the programme, a young woman called Fi who was thirty years old, discovered she had stage-4 ovarian cancer. She said, "I feel like death is sitting on my shoulder." What amazed me was not that she was quite candid about her experiences but that she could truthfully say, "Cancer is a gift." There is no doubt that Fi and her partner have had to face the brutal reality of gruesome chemotherapy and the impact this has had on their marriage. They will not be able to have children, to plan a longer life together. One day Fi's husband will wake up and find she is not beside him. Yet Fi will not let anyone cry around her, apart from her husband. She does not want people anticipating death – she wants them celebrating life.

It's not the best place to watch such a documentary. There is nowhere to hide when you have soggy eyes and a running nose on a plane. But the programme really challenged me. There are so many of us who are living a life we did not choose. These individuals did not necessarily know or believe in the God we know yet they were at peace taking each day at a time.

We sometimes find ourselves in the place where we don't expect to be. Instead of heading somewhere we are stopped at the junction of nowhere or heading over there when we don't want to be there in the first place. Maybe you are waiting to meet a life partner. Or you are someone who has never held a baby in your arms – one born of your womb. Perhaps your life has been ripped apart during the financial crisis and you are in a financial mess. Where you once had a nice house, car, and lifestyle you are now scraping money together to make ends meet. You can't tell anyone and you feel as if your life is not as you expected it to be. You are either waiting for something to happen or it has happened and it's not what you wanted.

What the Bible says about expectations

Perhaps you felt you had a calling into a certain type of work or ministry. Jonah was that man. The son of Amittai, Jonah's name means "dove". You may know him from the story of Jonah and the whale but his life has so much to teach us. In his later life we see that he was used by God to clearly speak and challenge one of Israel's worst kings – King Jeroboam II; this story is mentioned in 2 Kings 14:25. Israel was ruled by King Jeroboam II for about forty-one years. Although there was much prosperity in the kingdom and its borders had been extended there was great injustice. The people also turned away from God. It says in 2 Kings 14:24, "He did what was evil in the sight of the Lord."

God sent Amos and Hosea to challenge the king. He saw the distress of his people in Israel and spoke through Jonah, son of Amittai from Gath-hepher.

In the book of Jonah we get to know his character a little better. At the beginning of the story Jonah is commissioned by God to proclaim judgment to the 120,000 people of Nineveh. Jonah doesn't want to go as he believes he knows better. He is outraged that God wants to allow these people to experience His mercy. Jonah would have been brought up knowing that as a Jew he was part of God's chosen race. From an early age Jonah would know that the door to God's kingdom was not open to the Gentiles. You can understand his confusion. Instead of trusting God, however, Jonah decides to do things in his own way. God challenges his self-sufficiency, arrogance, and even his prejudice through what unfolds. Ultimately Jonah's unenthusiastic response to God leads to the salvation of Nineveh.

So Jonah heard God and tried to flee from Joppa (Jaffa is thirty miles north west of Jerusalem) to Tarsus in modern-day Turkey. He found a boat and paid for his fare out of the area. We know that we cannot flee form God. In this I am reminded of Psalm 139:1–12:

> *You have searched me, Lord,*
> *and you know me.*
> *You know when I sit and when I rise;*
> *you perceive my thoughts from afar.*
> *You discern my going out and my lying down;*
> *you are familiar with all my ways.*
> *Before a word is on my tongue*
> *you, Lord, know it completely.*
> *You hem me in behind and before,*
> *and you lay your hand upon me.*
> *Such knowledge is too wonderful for me,*
> *too lofty for me to attain.*
>
> *Where can I go from your Spirit?*
> *Where can I flee from your presence?*
> *If I go up to the heavens, you are there;*
> *if I make my bed in the depths, you are there.*
> *If I rise on the wings of the dawn,*
> *if I settle on the far side of the sea,*
> *even there your hand will guide me,*
> *your right hand will hold me fast.*
> *If I say, "Surely the darkness will hide me*
> *and the light become night around me,"*
> *even the darkness will not be dark to you;*
> *the night will shine like the day,*
> *for darkness is as light to you.*

God the creator of Heaven and Earth sent a storm. Even the sailors knew this was no ordinary storm but Jonah simply hid from the truth. Eventually the sailors pulled lots to find out who had offended God and thus caused the storm. Jonah was thrown into the sea and swallowed by a fish for three days and nights. We can read this in Jonah 1:17.

This story was a precursor to Jesus, who also asked God if this was the only way. Jesus questioned, prayed, and ultimately trusted God his Father.

Eventually the fish spewed Jonah onto dry land and he found shelter. Jonah did then go and speak to the people of Nineveh. They responded to God's mercy. Even the king of Nineveh took off his rich robes for sackcloth and ashes in repentance. God was able to use Jonah to reach the people of Nineveh despite his prejudices or stubbornness. Read Jonah 3:3. In fact Jonah did what was asked of him but he still felt that what he had been asked to do was wrong. He was so depressed about it that he said, "Now O Lord, please take my life from me, for it is better for me to die than to live."[1] God challenged Jonah but Jonah still did not understand God's mercy.

Jonah made himself a shelter east of the city and sat down. He wanted to see what would happen to Nineveh. God provided a leafy plant or bush to grow and provide him with shade. Jonah then became happy delighting in the plant and shade it brought. In fact he became so attached to his bush that when a worm destroyed it he was distraught. God challenged Jonah saying, "Is it right for you to be angry about a plant?"[2] God reminded Jonah that he was more concerned about the plant than the people of Nineveh.

Let's head back to Joppa for a minute. Peter had been in Joppa and Lydda sharing the gospel. In Joppa Peter prayed for a believer called Tabitha. Tabitha was well known for her kindness as she spent her time doing good helping the poor. When she fell ill the town was distraught and asked Peter to pray for her. God intervened and she woke from death. As many people came to faith and the church grew, Peter stayed with Simon the Tanner.

It was while Peter was resting that he had a vision of Heaven opening. There was a large sheet that lowered to earth by its four corners. In it were all kinds of animals from snakes to wild birds. Peter was told to kill and eat them. Peter, an adherent of the Jewish laws, told God he couldn't eat them as the animals were unclean. Again a voice spoke to him and told him that God had now declared they were clean. This was a huge change for Peter. While he was trying to understand what it meant, three men, guided by God's spirit, called on Peter to visit the Roman captain of the guard, Cornelius. Peter obeyed and shared the gospel message to Cornelius and the other Gentiles in Caesarea.

In Joppa God spoke to Peter challenging his prejudice and opened the doors to the Gentile world hearing about Jesus. Peter like Jonah would have been shaken by this revelation. Unlike Jonah he responded to God, trusting Him and doing it God's way. I would say that this was such a brave response from Peter. Later he headed to the apostles and the church in Jerusalem to share with them what had happened. They had been arguing about whether Peter could fraternize with non-circumcised believers or Gentiles. Peter's obedience and bravery brought criticism but also changed the church's response to the world outside Jerusalem. This was Peter; Peter who had denied Christ fearing for his own life, standing against the strength of the church in Jerusalem.

We don't always get what we want

The challenge for me was that there are times when I feel so passionate about something but yet God has a different plan. Let me try and illustrate this. If you asked me what I wanted to be as a child it would either be a nurse, writer, or artist. Then a couple of months before I came to a personal understanding of who Jesus is I had a dream.

In the dream I was working as a nurse in the Two-Thirds World. I realized that I wanted to work overseas. Maybe it was because I spent some of my childhood in Asia and had seen the poverty and injustice. Maybe it was because it was the time of Bob Geldoff, "Band Aid", and the terrible famines in Ethiopia. Then when I came to faith I was guided to train as a nurse. I then trained as a midwife with the plan to work on the mission field. I even applied to do work in Pokhara in Nepal as I finished my training but fell ill and could not go.[3] Every time I tried to push the door I discovered it was not the right time or something stopped me. Then came marriage, children, church life, and still the time was not right but the call never went away.

For my fortieth birthday we were able to go to Uganda as a family as part of a larger team. I knew I was in the right place. I have since had the amazing opportunities to visit a variety of places across the world teaching first aid, post abortion counselling, and resilience training. God has never taken away the call to work overseas – it just looks different to the way I would have thought it would look. God has been able to use my passion for these countries. In hindsight, if I had headed to Nepal when I wanted to go at twenty-one I would have had to leave early, perhaps broken by the experience. I have no doubt that it would have been a difficult experience spiritually, mentally, and physically.

On that same plane journey I was able to watch the recent film called *On Wings of Eagles* from Hong Kong director Stephen Shin. It has been called the "unofficial sequel" to Hugh Hudson's Oscar-winning 1981 film *Chariots of Fire*. Joseph Fiennes plays Eric Liddell, also known as the "Flying Scotsman". Eric Liddell was born in Tientsin, northern China, to Scottish missionaries. After his victory in the 400 m at the Paris Olympics in 1924 he returned to the land of his birth to serve the Chinese people. He taught the children of the wealthy parents believing that they would become the influential figures in China's future. He also used his athletic experience to train boys in a number of different sports. Then in 1943 he was interned in a Japanese prisoner of war camp as he insisted on staying with his Chinese family rather than escaping the Japanese invasion.

While there, Liddell organized the smuggling of food into the camp for the 2,000 starving inmates. He even refused an opportunity to leave the camp after Winston Churchill intervened on his behalf. He swapped his release for that of a pregnant prisoner instead. He died of a brain tumour aged forty-three, in Weifang in Shandong province, eastern China. He lived and died in China in a way others would not have expected. There is now a statue of the Flying Scotsman, Eric

Liddell, at the place where the camp was as Liddell became a religious and sporting hero in China after his selfless acts in the World War II internment camp.

Eric was brave. His life in China did not turn out as he expected. He had sent his wife and two girls to safety trusting he would be reunited with them. In his last letter to his wife, written on the day he died, Liddell wrote about his health as he thought he was suffering a nervous breakdown due to overwork. He actually had an inoperable brain tumour and died on 21 February 1945, five months before liberation.

There are so many ways that life does not play out as we might have expected it to. We have some wonderful friends, for example, who have such a special gift when around children but they have never had their own children. I also have some special friends who have never met a person they can marry and call husband or wife.

A few years ago my friend Cathy and I were talking about this as we commuted in and out of London. I was married with four teenagers and she had never been married. We both felt fulfilled in the roles and places we found ourselves in. We talked about our lives and laughed about the situations we found ourselves in. We journeyed in and out of London together sharing our life journeys. We decided that we would write a blog or emails between friends. One character was married with children, the other single. Recognize the scenario? And isn't life funnier than anything you can try and make up?

We soon realized that it would be a fun book that captured life. We had no answers to why a lot of things happen: why we sometimes end up in the life we did not expect or would choose.

Originally, when we sent in our manuscript to a publisher, we were asked if we could write a textbook about singleness. We couldn't. We felt we just did not have the answers. What we ended up doing is completing our novel which is called *Life Lines*.[5] We laughed and cried as we wrote it. We often wonder what the other people in the train thought of us as we both typed away. It really is a tongue-in-cheek look at life, but we lay down a challenge to ourselves and others: there are no real answers to some of these questions. We do know that one day we will have the answers and on that day nothing will matter as we will be with the One who loves us.

Psalm 27:1 says,

> *The Lord is my light and my salvation –*
> *whom shall I fear?*
> *The Lord is the stronghold of my life –*
> *of whom shall I be afraid?*

Prayer

Dear Father,

We thank You that You are the Lord of our lives. You are our light and salvation.

We can trust in You in whatever circumstance we find ourselves in.

Help us to trust You – that Your ways are higher than our ways.

Help us to be brave and respond to Your voice even when You have asked us to do things we don't expect.

Teach us to be brave and courageous.

In Jesus' name.

Amen.

CONCLUSION

Through this book we have been on a journey and have looked at the challenges of ill health, parenthood, retirement, and the unexpected life, to name a few. We have learned that bravery is courage for a season. We cannot predict what will come but we know that God is with us on this journey. We often have natural resilience and strength but God ultimately makes us brave. Throughout these pages we have seen that bravery has many faces.

Sometimes brave looks like stepping out of our comfort zone. We may feel lost and need a map but we have had the courage to step into new land or, like Peter, stepped out of the boat into the water. We simply have to listen to Jesus' voice. For others it may mean staying where you are: living out your life in quiet ways or sticking out difficult circumstances.

We are certainly all very different – different shapes and sizes living out different lives. Your picture of brave looks different from my picture of brave. You are remarkable. Some may be struggling each month to see if you have conceived a child in your womb, others have to endure lifelong illness. I don't know your challenges but I know for this season God can and has made you brave. We can trust Him. We can be quiet in His presence and He will refresh us. There will be times when you are afraid and don't feel brave just like I did waiting to see if I could go on my short-term mission trip.

Psalm 56:3–4 says, " When I am afraid I can trust in you… In God I trust and am not afraid."

Take hold of God's hand on this journey. You do not need to do this on your own. If you do not know the love of God then I would suggest that you get to know Him through His son Jesus Christ. He loves you; He is in this with you.

Prayer

Dear Lord,

I know that what I am going through is so different than those around me. They may not understand but You do. Knowing that You are on this journey with me means I can be brave. You make me brave.

Help me to live the life You want me to. Help me to trust You on a daily basis.

In Jesus' name.

Amen.

ENDNOTES

Acknowledgments

1. MAD stands for "Making a Difference". This charity is a community initiative linking South Buckinghamshire with a network of children's projects in Uganda. We aim to see our local area united and strengthened as we work together to change the lives of vulnerable children, improving their present situations and investing in their futures. MAD is about getting involved in something that's local, but that also positively impacts children in difficult circumstances thousands of miles away www.mad-bucks.co.uk/about/

Introduction

1. Thank you to Marilyn Glass and Paula Forber for your comments about being brave.

2. 2 Samuel 23:20.

Chapter 1

1. www.merriam-webster.com/dictionary/brave

2. http://dictionary.cambridge.org/dictionary/learner-english/brave_1

3. https://en.wikipedia.org/wiki/Brave

4. https://en.wikipedia.org/wiki/Bravery_(disambiguation)

5. www.independent.ie/irish-news/mystery-hero-revealed-student-describes-how-it-took-four-attempts-to-save-life-of-drowning-woman-trapped-in-car-35940609.html

6. www.independent.ie/irish-news/woman-hailed-a-hero-for-saving-child-3-who-slipped-into-river-when-she-was-looking-at-fish-34732667.html

7. www.dailymail.co.uk/news/article-4549694/Heroic-mother-saved-stranger-s-life-Manchester-blast.html

8. Mary Anne Radmacher, *Lean Forward into Your Life: Begin Each Day as if it Were On Purpose*, San Francisco, CA: Conari Press, 2007.

9. "The power of vulnerability"; see www.ted.com/talks/brene_brown_on_vulnerability

10. Plato, *The Republic*, translated by Allan Bloom, New York: Basic Books, 1968.

11. Douglas N. Walton, *Courage: A Philosophical Investigation*, Los Angeles: University of California Press, 1986.

12. Find his story in Judges 6.

Chapter 2

1. Stephen Jay Gould, *Dinosaur in a Haystack: Reflections in Natural History*, New York: Three Rivers Press, 1997. See chapter 4: "The Late Birth of a Flat Earth", pp. 38–50.

2. www.dailymail.co.uk/femail/food/article-1281455/Chip-chip-hooray-As-revealed-Britons-eat-16-types-chip-says-creative-kitchen.html

3. http://mingle-trend.respondi.com/uk/the-brits-love-affair-with-chips-shows-no-sign-of-waning/

4. "Bits and Pieces", 9 January 1992, pp. 13, 14, 15.

5. Caroline McClatchey, "How pasta became the world's favourite food", BBC News Online, 15 June 2011.

6. Ian Mortimer, "The ten greatest changes of the past 1000 years", 30 October 2014. www.theguardian.com/books/2014/oct/30/10-greatest-changes-of-the-past-1000-years

7. For more information see www.psychologytoday.com/conditions/adjustment-disorder

8. Debbie Duncan, *The Art of Daily Resilience*, Oxford: Monarch, 2017.

9. M. Goodyear and J. Mehmedovic, "5 Strategies for Leading Change",

Academic Impressions, April 2016; www.academicimpressions.com/news/5-strategies-leading-change

10. For more information see Parker J. Palmer, *Let Your Life Speak*, New York: John Wiley, 1999.

11. J. Austin and J. Bartunek, "Theories and Practice of Organization Development", *Handbook of Psychology*, Vol.12, 309–32, 2004.

12. Elisabeth Kübler-Ross and David Kessler, *On Grief and Grieving: Finding the Meaning of Grief Through the Five Stages of Loss*, Scribner, 2007.

13. 2 Corinthians 3:18; Ephesians 4:11–16.

14. Hebrews 13:5; Deuteronomy 31:8.

15. O. Prochaska and C. C. DiClemente, "The Transtheoretical Approach", in J. C. Norcross and M. R. Goldfried (eds), *Handbook of Psychotherapy Integration*, 2nd edn, New York: OUP, 2005, pp. 147–71.

16. Romans 8:28; Psalm 90:15.

Chapter 3

1. www.huffingtonpost.com/lisa-copen/is-being-brave-in-the-fac_b_769943.html

2. The King's Fund, "Long-term conditions and multi-morbidity", 2017: www.kingsfund.org.uk/time-to-think-differently/trends/disease-and-disability/long-term-conditions-multi-morbidity

3. Department of Health, *Long Term Conditions Compendium of Information*, 3rd edn, 2012. Available at www.gov.uk/government/uploads/system/uploads/attachment_data/file/216528/dh_134486.pdf

4. T. Vos, R. M. Barber, B. Bell et al., "Global, regional, and national incidence, prevalence, and years lived with disability for 301 acute and chronic diseases and injuries in 188 countries, 1990–2013: A Systematic Analysis for the Global Burden of Disease Study", *Lancet*, 2013; 386 (9995): 743–800.

5. S. McManus, P. Bebbington, R. Jenkins, T. Brugha T. (eds), *Mental health and wellbeing in England: Adult Psychiatric Morbidity Survey 2014*, Leeds: NHS Digital, 2016.

6. The author discusses this topic in her previous book *The Art of Daily Resilience*, Oxford: Monarch, 2017.

7. Taken from Emm Roy's *The First Step*, and quoted at www.goodreads.com/work/quotes/42231869-the-first-step

8. www.premierchristianity.com/Blog/What-not-to-say-to-those-with-chronic-illness-and-5-ways-to-help

9. Name changed to preserve confidentiality.

10. www.inf.org/our-work/green-pastures-hospital/

11. For example, see Philippians 1:29; 1 Peter 2:21 or 2 Timothy 3:12.

12. William H. Frey, Denise Desota-Johnson, Carrie Hoffman, John T. McCall, "Effect of stimulus on the chemical composition of human tears", *American Journal of Ophthalmology* 1981; 92 (4): 559–67.

13. www.huffingtonpost.com/lisa-copen/is-being-brave-in-the-fac_b_769943.html

Chapter 4

1. B. Wymbs and W. Pelham, "Rate and predictors of divorce among parents of youths with ADHD", *Journal of Consulting and Clinical Psychology*, 2008; 76(5): 735–44.

2. R. Urbano and R. Hodapp, "Divorce in Families of Children with Down Syndrome: A Population-Based Study", *American Journal on Mental Retardation*, 2007; 112(4): 261–74.

3. S. Swaminathan, G. R. Alexander, S. Boulet, "Delivering a very low birth weight infant and the subsequent risk of divorce or separation", *Maternal and Child Health Journal* 2006; 10(6): 473–79.

4. S. L. Hartley, E. T. Barker, M. M. Seltzer et al., "The relative risk and timing of divorce in families of children with an autism spectrum disorder", *Journal of Family Psychology*, 2010; 24(4): 449–57.

5. Debra Ginsberg, *Raising Blaze: A Mother and Son's Long, Strange Journey into Autism*, New York: Harper Perennial, 2003, p. 188.

6. www.ons.gov.uk/peoplepopulationandcommunity/
birthsdeathsandmarriages/families/bulletins/familiesandhousehol
ds/2015-11-05

7. L. Dennerstein, E. Dudley and J. Guthrie, "Empty nest or revolving door? A prospective study of women's quality of life in midlife during the phase of children leaving and re-entering the home", *Psychological Medicine* 2002; 32(3): 545–50.

8. E. B. Harkins, "Effects of empty nest transition on self-report of psychological and physical well-being", *Journal of Marriage and the Family* 1978; 40(3): 549–56; M. F. Lowenthal and D. Chiriboga, "Transition to the empty nest: Crisis, challenge, or relief?", *Archives of General Psychiatry* 1972; 26(1): 8–14.

9. www.independent.co.uk/student/news/cant-cook-wont-cook-a-tenth-of-students-never-make-their-own-food-8794409.html

10. www.telegraph.co.uk/news/uknews/1467748/Why-students-cant-cook-wont-cook.html

Chapter 5

1. J. I. Packer, *Finishing Our Course with Joy*, Crossway: USA, 2014.

Chapter 6

1. Paula Banks, "Sandwich Generation Stress: 6 Ways to Cope While Raising Kids and Caring for Elderly Parents"; see www.empoweringparents.com/article/sandwich-generation-stress-6-ways-to-cope-while-raising-kids-and-caring-for-elderly-parents/

2. Australian Bureau of Statistics 2012, "Providing primary care to a person with a disability", in 4125.0 *Gender Indicators, Australia*, January 2012.

3. K. Parker and E. Paton "The Sandwich Generation", January 2013, www.pewsocialtrends.org/2013/01/30/the-sandwich-generation/

4. See www.sandwichgeneration.com/

5. K. Parker and E. Paton "The Sandwich Generation", January 2013, www.pewsocialtrends.org/2013/01/30/the-sandwich-generation/

Chapter 7

1. T. Scotland and S. Heys, *Understanding the Ypres Salient: An Illuminating Battlefield Guide*, Solihull: Helion & Company, 2017.

2. Allan Hall, "Mustard gas blisters and a daily risk of death: Bravery of soldiers still clearing the 'iron harvest' of World War 1 shells beneath Flanders' fields", *Daily Mail*, 10 November 2013.

3. Anon., *A War Nurse's Diary: Sketches from a Belgian Field Hospital*, Pickle Partners Publishing, 2013.

Chapter 8

1. Ian Smith, "South Vietnam, 9 June 1972, Nick Ut", *New Statesman*, 1 April 2010.

2. F. Luskin, "What is Forgiveness?", *Greater Good Magazine*, 19 August 2010, https://greatergood.berkeley.edu/article/item/what_is_forgiveness

3. Desmond Tutu, "Truth and Reconciliation", *Greater Good Magazine*, 1 September 2004, https://greatergood.berkeley.edu/article/item/truth_and_reconciliation

Chapter 9

1. www.beliefnet.com/prayers/catholic/comfort/show-me-the-course.aspx

2. F. Holböck, *Married Saints and Blesseds Through the Centuries*, San Francisco: Ignatius Press, 2012.

3. Benedict XVI, General audience, St Peter's Square, Wednesday 9 April 2008.

4. Acts 17:6–9.

Chapter 10

1. D. Duncan, *The Art of Daily Resilience*, Oxford: Monarch, 2017.

2. J. Bowlby, "Processes of Mourning", *International Journal of Psychoanalysis*, 42, 317–39, 1961.

3. C. Parkes, *Bereavement: Studies of Grief in Adult Life*, London:

Tavistock, 1972 and C. M. Parkes, and R. S. Weiss, *Recovery from Bereavement*, New York: Basic Books, 1983.

4. Molly Fumia, *Safe Passages*, York Beach, ME: Conari Press, 1983.

5. Dr B. Kellemen, *A Biblical Model of Grieving*, RPM Ministries, 2010. www.rpmministries.org/2010/07/a-biblical-model-of-grieving/

6. Calvin's Commentaries, "A Harmony of the Gospels", 3:313, Grand Rapids: Baker.

7. Genesis 35:8.

8. J. K. Doka (ed), *Disenfranchised Grief:* Lexington, MA: Lexington Books, 1989.

9. Psalm 23 taken from *The Message*.

Chapter 11

1. Jonah 3:3.

2. Jonah 4:9.

3. Actually, years later, I was able to go to Nepal with International Nepal Fellowship and visited the hospital where I would have been based.

4. D. Duncan and C. Le Feuvre, *Life Lines*, Authentic Media: 2015.